Beyond the Cascade

Step-by-Step Guides to 88 Classic 3-Ball Juggling Tricks

The Ugly Juggling Company
Newcastle Upon Tyne, U.K.

First edition1990. Printed in the United States of America.
Second edition 1993.
Reprinted 1994.

Designed and Typeset by Keepdate Publishing,
21 Portland Terrace, Jesmond, Newcastle Upon Tyne NE2 1QQ.

Printed in Great Britain at The Alden Press, Oxford.

ISBN 0-9516998-1-4

Dedication

To my seven-year-old son, Tavet, already a remarkable juggler; to my wife, Reina, for her belief and encouragement; to Larry, for his great array of skills as juggler, editor, and collaborator – and to that great group of "3-ball people" everywhere!

Contents

Foreword

Shortly after I began juggling four years ago, I became obsessed with learning Mills' Mess – arguably the most elegant three-ball trick in existence. But even after months of frustrating effort, I still couldn't figure out the trick. Then, fortunately, I met George Gillson. He gave me a sheet of paper with his step-by-step description of Mills' Mess. Within a week, I clearly understood the Mess, and within a month I could do four or five relatively smooth repetitions of the trick. What a feeling! I'd taken a giant step "Beyond the Cascade."

Reasoning that if even I – the world's least gifted juggler – could learn a difficult trick like Mills' Mess using his instructions, others might be able to do the same, I urged George to diagram all the best tricks he knew. He did, and then we both sought out the best 3-ball tricks we could find, and pretty soon we had a complete book manuscript, the printed version of which you now hold in your hand.

As the instigator and editor of "Beyond the Cascade," I became the first person to benefit from George's elegantly simple notation system. I remain a complete klutz; nevertheless, my 3-ball juggling has improved remarkably as I've worked on this book. Since you are certainly better prepared than I to take advantage of the instruction in this book, let me be the first to congratulate you on the new level of 3-ball excellence you are about to attain.

Larry Swanson
Publisher
Cascade Books

Introduction

If you have already made a start in 3-ball juggling, this is the book for you. It assumes that you can do at least a Cascade, and maybe a 3-Ball Shower, perhaps in both directions. You have mastered some 2-in-1-Hand patterns, and your behind-the-back throws are coming along nicely. You're not a rank beginner anymore and you're eager for new challenges. This book should answer that need.

If you **are** a rank beginner, this may still be the book for you. In Chapter 1, I present five tricks that will teach you basic 3-ball juggling skills and prepare you for the more advanced tricks that complete the book. (Even if you're an experienced 3-ball juggler, you might want to review these tricks to get acquainted with my step-by-step system of presenting the tricks.)

For me, the most exciting thing about juggling is spotting a terrific new trick – one that not only looks great, but seems within reach of, or not too much beyond, my current level of skill. Then I can't wait for some free time to try it. In parks, gymnasiums, and on street corners, I'm always hoping to catch a juggler in action, watch his or her routine, and, if possible, start a conversation exchanging ideas about tricks and variations. And though often I need some time to get a trick right, I can fairly say I've mastered a good number of them.

Three-ball tricks are my favourite kind of juggling, and for those who share this affection, I've collected the best patterns, variations, fakes, stops, and starts that I've encountered, or, in some instances, invented – nearly 100 tricks in all. Since I've included mostly tricks that, to my knowledge, won't be found in any other book on juggling, I bet you'll find at least 50, or maybe even more, that you've either never seen performed or have seen but were not exactly sure what the juggler was doing.

To make learning the tricks as easy as possible, each throw and each catch is described step by step, with accompanying step-by-step diagrams. In this way you can almost see the trick slowly unfolding – like watching slow-motion or, even better, a stop-motion juggling act. This allows you to study and re-study the moves, trying them over and over, until finally you've established the requisite motor skills and the trick begins to work.

Some of the patterns are easy, others are moderately difficult, and some will seem almost impossible to learn. The step-by-step approach, plus some persistence, should make it possible for you to master all of them, and soon you'll be amazing your friends – and even yourself – with some very classy 3-ball manoeuvres.

As drawn, the diagrams in this book represent what you, the juggler, see as you execute the trick, and the balls are numbered in the sequence in which they are thrown. I've presented all the tricks with a right-handed juggler in mind, my assumption being that, for quicker learning, the stronger hand should be given the more difficult assignment. My apologies to the lefties. I'm left-handed myself, so, obviously, my choice comes only from the need for a uniform approach and is **not** a matter of dextrophilic prejudice. Besides, for greater all-around skill and control, it's a good idea to learn to do the tricks with both hands anyway.

I hope these tricks satisfy your yearning for new juggling adventures and that you enjoy learning them. If you have a terrific 3-ball trick that you think I might not know about, drop me a line c/o The Ugly Juggling Company. I'm putting together a new collection and it's always exciting to hear about another really fabulous 3-ball move.

George Gillson

Chapter 1

Basic Patterns

If you are just getting started in juggling, here are five basic patterns that are the groundwork for learning the more advanced tricks presented later in these pages. You'll want to master them before you move on to Chapter 2. They are beautiful patterns in themselves and quite worthy of showing off to your friends. When you've got them working smoothly, you can consider yourself a bona fide juggler.

The Cascade

You can begin to learn the Cascade with the following practice pattern, called, for obvious reasons, the Two-Ball Exchange.

THE TWO-BALL EXCHANGE

Using just two balls, one in each hand, hold them out in front of you, forearms parallel to the ground, about the way you would hold the edges of a tray. Then...

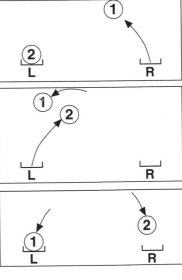

1. RH throws ① over towards the LH. (Don't worry about how your hand throws the ball or how it catches it. Just send it in an arc, about head-high, aimed to drop into the LH at the edge of the "tray.")

2. When ① peaks, LH throws ② in an arc toward the RH.

3. Finally, LH catches ① and, a split-second later, RH catches ②. The two balls have been exchanged.

To get controlled, even throws, practice a bit with just one ball, sending it back and forth in head-high arcs and concentrating on a consistent height; then go back to two balls. When you can do the Two-Ball Exchange smoothly, switch the order – that is, throw ① first with the left hand and then ② with the right hand.

THE CASCADE

When you can do the Two-Ball Exchange competently, beginning with either hand, you are, believe it or not, ready to juggle three balls. Hold two balls in your right hand, one in your left. Then…

1. RH throws ① over toward the left.

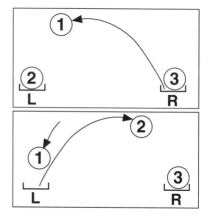

2. As ① peaks, LH throws ② over toward the right, and catches ①.

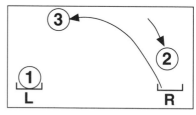

3. As ② peaks, RH throws ③ over toward the left, and catches ②.

4. As ③ peaks, LH throws ① over toward the right and catches ③ and then – could it be? Yes! – you're juggling! To be specific, you're doing the Cascade.

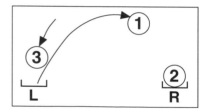

Introducing "Scoop"–In the Cascade, as in many juggling patterns, your hands will make a scooping motion as you execute the trick. As you do the Cascade, for example, you catch each ball at the outside edge of the juggle space and "scoop" the ball in a small arc toward the middle of the space to throw it, and then return your hand to the outside of the juggle space to make your next catch.

Here's the path that the balls follow in the Cascade. Notice that each throw goes **underneath** the ball that is peaking and about to be caught. This observation leads us to our next basic pattern – the Reverse Cascade.

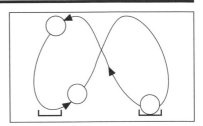

The Reverse Cascade

This juggle employs exactly the same exchange principle as the Cascade, but now each throw will be directed **over** (or "outside" of) the ball about to be caught, and aimed so as to fall down through the **middle** (or "inside") of the juggle space.

The flow path looks like this, with the balls being thrown up on the **outside** of the pattern:

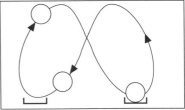

When you do a regular Cascade, your hands catch each ball on the outside and "scoop" toward the middle of the juggle space as they make their tosses. To do the Reverse Cascade, you'll have to reverse the scoop – that is, you'll catch each ball in the middle and scoop toward the outside of the juggle space to make the throw.

* *

Juggling is great exercise – in fact,
I almost called this book "Pumping Beanbags".

* *

The Shower

When "Showering," all the balls are thrown with the same hand, caught with the other hand, and then sent with a short horizontal toss back to the throwing hand – a one-way, roughly circular pattern, in which each ball follows exactly the same path.

At first, you might want to try showering with just two balls to get the feeling of the initial high throw and the low, horizontal return toss. When you can shower two balls smoothly, advance to three.

To shower three balls, hold ① and ② in the RH and ③ in the LH.

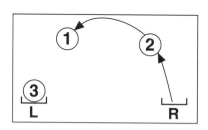

1. RH, with a high arcing throw, tosses ① toward the left, then, quickly, follows with ②.

2. LH makes a short horizontal toss of ③ over to the RH, then catches ①, tosses it across, catches ②, tosses it across, and so on. Meanwhile, RH throws every ball as soon as it's passed across. Continue until the phone rings or you drop a ball, whichever comes first.

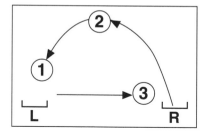

The Half Shower

The Shower is a rather fast juggle. The Half Shower slows the tempo considerably by replacing the straight horizontal toss with a short upward lob.

The balls still follow a one- way "circular" path, but the circle now has an upward bulge where the lob occurs. Here's what the pattern looks like:

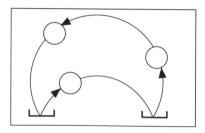

2-in-1-Hand

This juggle uses two balls and only one (either) hand. There are three 2-in-1-hand patterns: "columns," in which the two balls are thrown alternately straight up and down next to one another, and the "clockwise" and "counterclockwise" patterns, in which the two balls follow each other in a circular path.

Try the "columns" pattern first. With two balls in the RH...

RH throws ① straight up about a foot, then throws ② straight up—same height—next to ① (either side) and catches ① as it falls. RH then immediately throws ① straight back up again and catches ②, throws ② up and catches ①, and so on.

Keep the paths of the balls **side by side** and **not** one in front of the other; you want your audience to see clearly what's happening.

When you've got the columns pattern working, try sending the balls in a continuous clockwise or counter-clockwise direction. For a clockwise juggle, RH throws each ball from the centre in an arc toward the right, makes all catches at the right and carries each ball back to the centre for the next throw. For a counter-clockwise juggle, RH throws each ball from the right and makes all catches in the centre.

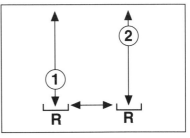

COLUMNS

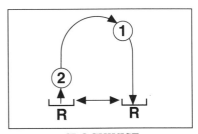

CLOCKWISE

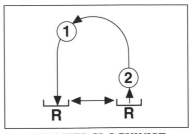

COUNTERCLOCKWISE

Chapter 2

Beyond the Basics: Cascade Variations

If you've mastered the Cascade and the other basic patterns in Chapter 1, you've taught yourself a lot more than you realise. You now have a repertoire of specific motor reflexes that will click into action at the precise moment you need them – without your even knowing what's happening! For instance, in the Cascade variations that follow, a pattern may require that your right hand send a ball along a new and unfamiliar trajectory. Scary! But don't panic; part of your mind (the part you developed learning the basic tricks in Chapter 1) recognises the situation, automatically starts tracking the ball, and gets your left hand in place for the usual Cascade catch. And when you make that catch, no one will be more surprised than you!

Honing one's motor skills is a major part of the fun of juggling. It's like dancing – once you've learned the basic steps, you just launch yourself into it and let your body take over. Now that you're an accomplished Cascader, try the following "fancy steps" and launch yourself "Beyond the Cascade."

Clawing

A great basic Cascade variation! Instead of waiting for a ball to drop into your hand, you "claw" it – reaching up as it peaks and pulling it down in a catlike clawing motion. You can do this just once for a surprise effect, or do three or four successive Claws, or claw continuously in a two-handed Claw Cascade. In this latter pattern, the palms will face downward, even when you throw, and you'll find that, though the Claw **catches** are easy, controlling the palm-down **throws** will require practice. At first, try consecutive Claw catches and throws with just one hand while the other hand cascades normally; then switch over. Later on, when you can claw reasonably well, try the Claw variation of the Straight-Out Cascade (p. 7).

Straight-out Cascade

The more variations of the Cascade the better, so add these three to your repertoire.

STRAIGHT-OUT CASCADE

Throw each ball up and out from the centre of your body – the belt buckle (to pinpoint the exact anatomical location) – catch each with the opposite hand, and carry it straight back in for a new throw. A fountain effect is created – every ball pops up and out, falls, and is carried back in, along a circular track perpendicular to your chest.

STRAIGHT-IN CASCADE

Here the balls fly toward you, being thrown from a distant point up and in toward the centre of the body, to be caught just in front of (and be careful not to injure) your belt buckle.

STRAIGHT-OUT CLAWING

For the toughest challenge, do the Straight-Out Cascade, but "claw" each catch and keep your palm turned downward as you throw. Of the three Straight-Out variations, this is by far the most dynamic.

Tennis

In this pattern, one ball – the "tennis" ball – flies back and forth over the juggle space the same way that the ball in a tennis game flies back and forth over the net. To do this, cascade, and then make one Reverse Cascade throw (the "tennis" throw) for every two regular Cascade throws.

Cascade, then...

1. RH cascades, LH cascades, then RH **reverse** cascades ("tennises" the ball over the juggle).

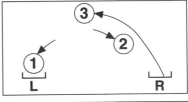

2. LH cascades, RH cascades, LH **reverse** cascades (tennises the ball back over the juggle).

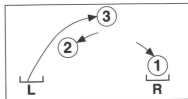

The Reverse Cascade throws keep the "tennis" ball (always the same ball) oscillating in its own simple little juggle seemingly independent of the other two balls, a surprising and amusing effect.

Three-ball Flash

Cascade three balls in a normal pattern. Then, starting with either hand, and maintaining the same speed of throwing (a quick 1-2-3 pace), send three consecutive tosses up about 8 or 10 feet in the air. The balls follow a regular Cascade pattern, only at a greater height. There will be a slight wait for the balls to descend – some jugglers use this pause to clap their hands one or more times. Then catch them 1-2-3 as they fall and resume a normal-level Cascade.

You might want to start the Flash with either the right or the left hand. Throwing the sequences R-L-R and L-R-L, you'll discover that these are two different skills. You might also try alternating Flashes—three high tosses, three low tosses, three high, three low, and so on. Or, try the most difficult pattern: all high, quick three-ball sequences—R-L-R, pause, L-R-L, pause, R-L-R, pause, and so on. As you might guess, throws of **uniform height** are the desired goal. (See also Chapter 7, "Beyond Three Balls.")

Cross-arm Cascade

First, cross one forearm over the other (either left over right or right over left). Keep your forearms parallel to the ground, as you would if you were doing a normal juggle. Now, whichever hand holds two balls throws first. Use Reverse Cascade throws—that is, throw each ball from the outside edge of the pattern, aiming, more or less, for the centre. For the first few seconds, you'll probably be totally paralysed with a "crossed-wires" kind of confusion. Take those few seconds to breathe, relax, centre yourself, visualise, concentrate, motivate, and then – throw that first ball!

The Carry Under

This crossed-arm trick features a repeating carry that is timed to swoop under and just miss a ball descending in the opposite direction. Sound interesting?

Here are the details: You start with two balls in the right hand, one in the left hand, **arms crossed, right over left**. Throughout the juggle the left hand remains at the right. The right hand, however, oscillates in a sort of circular movement, throwing every ball, cross-armed, from the **left**, but making all catches at the **right**.

After each catch, completing the circle, the right hand carries the ball back to the cross-arm position. It's this swoop under a dropping ball that gives the trick its essential charm. The trick has a complicated look, but Step 1 is just a starting move and, in fact, just two moves – Steps 2 and 3 – make up the entire pattern.

Start with ① and ③ in the right hand, ② in the left, arms crossed, right over left. Then...

1. RH throws ① in an arc over toward the right.

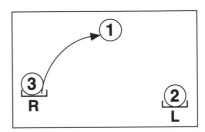

2. LH tosses ② straight up and catches ①.

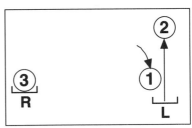

3. RH (still on the left side) throws ③ to the right in the same arc as the throw in Step 1, then goes right to catch the descending ②. Then it carries ② back to the left, swooping under the airborne ③.

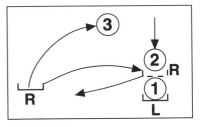

(NOTE: The right arm always crosses over the left.)

Now the left hand repeats Step 2, the right hand repeats Step 3, and you're off and swooping!

Carry to the Opposite Elbow

This is a very busy trick – with carries, under-the-arm throws, and claw catches – and, therefore, highly impressive. Here's how it works. On every third throw, a ball is carried to a point just in front of the elbow of the opposite arm where it is released in a short throw straight up – that's the basic effect of the trick. But in addition, all right hand tosses will be made on the **left** side and all left hand tosses will be made on the **right** side! (No wonder they call it juggling!)

Start with a Cascade, then...

1. LH swoops under the right arm and throws ① straight up at the far right side of the juggle, then, back left, catches the ball RH just threw.

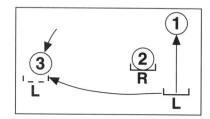

2. As LH goes **under** (see Step 1 diagram), RH simultaneously carries ② **over** to a point just in front of the left elbow, tosses it straight up (with a claw throw) and swings right-ward, over, and down to make a claw-catch of ①.

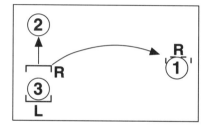

3. LH tosses ③ straight up at the right middle of the juggle space and catches ② at the left.

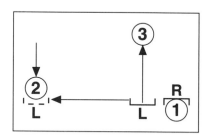

4. RH, continuing the claw-catch movement (from Step 2), swoops down and under the left arm to toss ① straight up at the far left side of the juggle; then catches ③ back at the right middle.

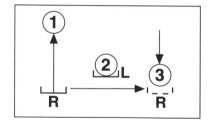

5. As RH goes **under**, LH simultaneously carries ② **over** to a point just in front of the right elbow, tosses it straight up (with a claw throw) and swings leftward over and down to make a claw-catch of ①.

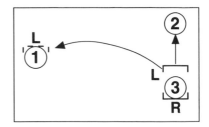

6. RH tosses ③ straight up at the left middle of the juggle space and catches ② at the right.

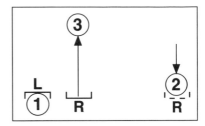

Repeat Steps 1-6.

Flash and Cross-arm Cascade

Put the Cascade, Three-Ball Flash, and Cross-Arm Cascade together and the result is an exciting and flashy variation to add sparkle to your routine. First, cascade. Then send the balls up in a Flash, throwing the third ball straight up the middle. Now, cross your arms and catch the the first two balls as they fall and as the last ball drops begin a Reverse Cascade **with your arms crossed**!

Catch under the Hand

A surprise catch is featured here – while cascading, one ball is thrown wide, **over** the opposite hand, and you then reach way **under** that hand to make the catch. It's the kind of frantic, last-second save that Buster Keaton would have liked. Start with a Cascade, then…

1. RH tosses ① in an arc that will carry it about 2 or 3 inches beyond the usual point in space for a LH catch, and catches the incoming ball, ②.

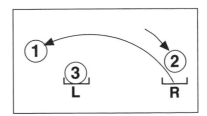

2. RH immediately throws **again**, sending ② right after ①, but this time aiming for a **normal** LH catch; then RH reaches **under** the LH to catch ① as it drops on the far left side and carries it back to the right.

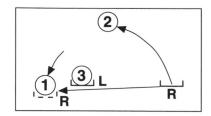

3. LH tosses ③, catches ②, and, if you choose, you can resume the Cascade. Or (when you're ready)...

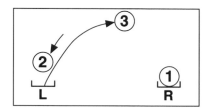

You can expand the pattern and make under-the-hand catches on **both** sides of the juggle by following Steps 1-3 with...

4. RH cascades ①, catches ③. This completes a four-toss series. Now reverse Steps 1-4.

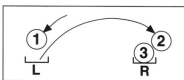

5. LH wide toss over RH.

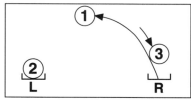

6. LH regular toss and reach under RH to make the catch.

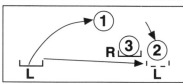

7. RH cascade and catch.

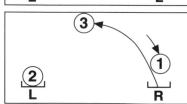

8. LH cascade and catch. And so on...

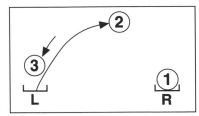

And, for a really fast-moving action juggle, do Steps 1 and 2 (the two consecutive RH throws) like this...

1. RH wide toss (and catch).

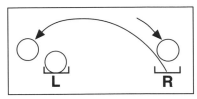

2. RH regular toss and reach under LH to make the catch.

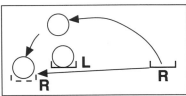

Then immediately do Steps 5 and 6 (the two consecutive LH throws)...

5. LH wide toss (and catch).

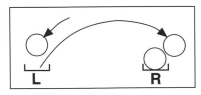

6. LH regular toss and reach under RH to make the catch.

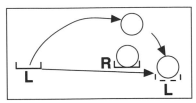

By eliminating the normal Cascade tosses in Steps 3 and 4 and 7 and 8, you increase the tempo **and the humour** in this juggle. As you lunge for those far-side, under-the-hand catches, it looks like you're gonna "lose it" any second.

Reachover

When doing a Cascade, any variation, however slight, can create instant mystification, causing your audience's collective jaw to drop. In the Reachover, for instance, instead of the usual Cascade throw across the body, you make a low toss, **straight up**. The opposite hand then has to **reach over** to get the ball. It's a simple move, but when you spring this subtle and unexpected change-up, eyes will widen in the classical "Wuddy do?!" response, and it will warm your juggler's heart.

Cascade, then...

1. LH throws ① straight up about 8 inches and catches the ball incoming from the right.

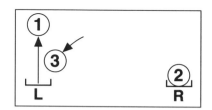

2. RH releases ② with a normal throw but continues the arm motion to reach over and catch ① as it peaks.

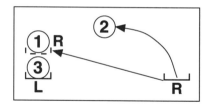

3. LH moves right-ward and tosses ③ under the reaching RH, then catches incoming ②, while...

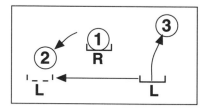

4. RH carries ① back to a normal throwing position and continues the Cascade.

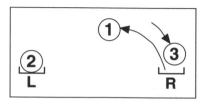

After you get the move working smoothly, try the Reachover, Claw, and Whiparound (p. 95), a more complicated variation of this trick.

You can also expand the Reachover by doing alternate **right-** and **left-side** reaching. Do Steps 1, 2, and 3, then continue with the reverse of these steps for 4, 5, and 6. That is...

4. RH carries ① back to a normal throwing position, then throws ① straight up about 8 inches and catches the ball incoming from the left.

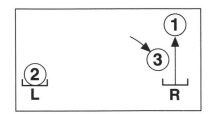

5. LH releases ② in a normal throw but continues the arm motion to reach over and catch ① as it peaks.

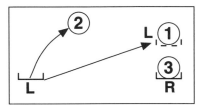

6. RH tosses ③ under the reaching LH and catches incoming ②.

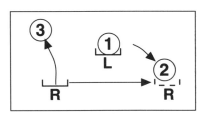

7. LH carries ① back to a normal throwing position and either resumes the Cascade or starts a new cycle with a straight-up throw as in Step 1. (In this diagram, the Cascade is resumed.)

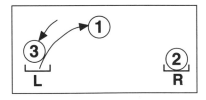

* *

The mind is amazing. It starts to work the
minute you're born and never stops
until you try to juggle.

* *

Reachunder

This move is more than just a variation of the Reach**over**. The Reach**under**'s key feature – a throw straight up **that is allowed to drop low enough for an under-the-arm catch**(!)—creates a distinctly new juggle with a personality all its own. And, as you shall see, the Reachunder then leads to another fascinating variation as well.

Start with the Cascade pattern. Then...

1. Instead of a regular throw, LH tosses ① up a few inches and slightly to the **left** (!) and catches the ball incoming from the right.

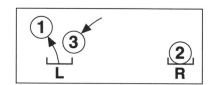

2. RH cascades ② to the left and then reaches under the left arm to catch ① descending at the far left.

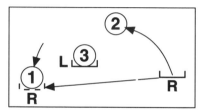

3. LH, meanwhile, has carried ③ to the centre of the juggle space and tosses it short and low to the right, then goes back left to catch ②.

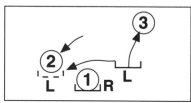

4. RH tosses ① straight up the middle, then catches ③ just to the right.

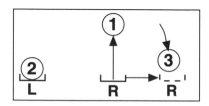

Now repeat Steps 1-4, and so on.

The variation on the Reachunder that I mentioned above is achieved by simply changing Step 4 to produce a wonderful circling effect – a total transformation of the original pattern.

Here's the change:

4. RH, having just caught ① at the far left (Step 2), carries it low to the right and continues the circular movement with a reverse cascade toss of ① to the left; then catches ③ at the right middle.

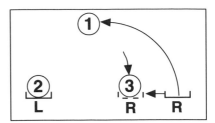

* *

I'll never forget September 30, 1982...
the day I made my debris in juggling.

* *

Chops

Chops is a speedy, hard-to-learn, but highly satisfying juggle wherein each ball is **carried** in a fast diagonal "chop" from in front of one shoulder down and across the body to a point low on the opposite side. From here, a throw is made straight up. The left hand throws straight up on right side, and the right hand throws straight up on left. Visualise this: Two consecutive Chops – one with each hand – together form an X, and the two straight-up throws, one on each side of the juggle space, are parallel to each other, like the vertical sides of a box. This trick combines these relatively simple moves to create an exciting, fast-moving three-ball pattern (which is particularly effective with clubs).

Cascade, and when it's time for a right hand throw...

1. RH reaches under the left arm and throws ① straight up the left side of the juggle space, then moves back to the right to catch ③. Meanwhile, LH is raising ② to shoulder height.

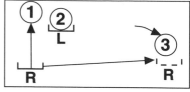

2. LH "chops" (carries) ② down and across to the right and makes a throw straight up the right side of the juggle space. Note that the throwing motion will bring the LH up and back to the left for a **shoulder-high catch** of ①. At the same time that LH is throwing ② up...

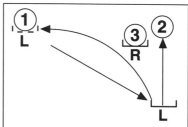

3. RH chops ③ down and across to the left, under the left arm, and makes a throw straight up the left side of the juggle space, and moves up and back to the right for a shoulder-high catch of ②.

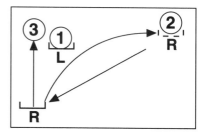

Continue by alternating Steps 2 and 3. Note that as one hand throws, the other simultaneously chops. Also, each shoulder-high catch automatically places the hand in position for the next chop.

Clawed Chops

No, Clawed Chops is not an old movie actor. It's what happens when you do Chops with your palms facing downward on **all** throws and catches. Surprisingly, the clawing totally transforms the Chops pattern, because the two hands move side by side – one carrying, the other clawing – throughout the juggle, which does not happen with Chops. As you will see, this new tandem action creates a unique and exciting effect.

There are just two moves to learn, but, like Chops, they're speedy and energetic to the point of being positively aerobic. So, while you might feel frustrated about getting this trick to work, console yourself – the exercise benefits will be immediate and substantial.

Start with a Cascade and when it's time for a RH toss...

1a. RH, with a claw throw under the left arm, tosses ① straight up on the **left** side, then swings over to the right to claw the ball thrown previously – let's call it ③.

1b. As the RH swings under it, LH carries ② on an arc up, over, and down the centre of the juggle space, timed so as to follow along next to the RH as it swings over and claws ③.

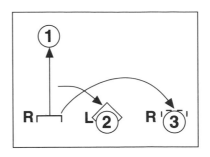
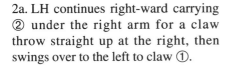

2a. LH continues right-ward carrying ② under the right arm for a claw throw straight up at the right, then swings over to the left to claw ①.

2b. As the LH swings under it, RH carries ③ on an arc up, over, and down the centre of the juggle space, timed so as to follow along next to the LH as it swings over and claws ①.

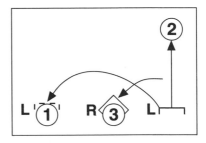

Continue the pattern by alternating Steps 1 and 2.

* *

In juggling you must educate your muscles...
it's mind over motor.

* *

Chapter 3

Mills' Mess

Said the doc to the lad,
" 'Tis my guess,
That you've thrown out both
shoulders, no less.
Tell me, how did you manage
To do so much damage?"
Said the lad, " I was tryin'
Mills' Mess."

George Gillson

The distinctive features of Mills' Mess – the crossing and uncrossing arms, the "back-tosses," under-the-arm catches, and, particularly, the "toss-catch-and-carry" move – combine to form a smoothly flowing pattern of almost hypnotic complexity. It is a truly unique juggle, well deserving of its popularity.

The Cross-Arm Cascade (p. 8) and the group of tricks presented here – besides being terrific moves in and of themselves – each have some element of Mills' Mess in them, and thus provide an excellent preparation for the upcoming challenge of Mills' Mess at the end of this chapter.

Spiral†

Here's a way to get all three balls circling in the same direction – like a spiral or the cars on a Ferris wheel.

Start with two balls in the left hand, one in the right, both hands at the right side of the juggle space.

1. LH back-tosses ① up and toward the left – in a counterclockwise direction.

2. RH tosses ② toward the left with a reverse cascade throw, and, reaching over the left arm, immediately catches ① at far left and carries it, continuing the counterclockwise circular motion, back to the right.

3. LH, from under the right arm, back-tosses ③ up and toward the left and immediately catches ② and carries it, continuing the counterclockwise circular motion, back to the right.

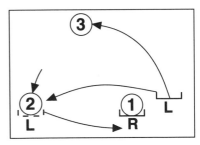

Now, just keep repeating Steps 2 and 3. All throws are made on the right side of the pattern. All catches are made on the left side and immediately carried back to the right. All left hand throws will seem to come from **under** the right arm as that arm reaches over to make its catches.

---

†Since the balls move around in a circle but aren't actually thrown in a shower pattern, some jugglers call this move "The False Shower".

Pistons

In this trick, as in Mills' Mess and similar patterns, the hands keep crossing and uncrossing. However, unlike those more advanced moves, there are **no carries** in Pistons. The hands cross to make catches, but **each ball remains in the same column throughout**, popping straight up and down. The juggle has a 6-step cycle, the tosses settling into a left-middle-right, left-middle-right sequence. Of course, this order can be reversed, as can the way the arms cross (left over right, or right over left), as you will see.

Start with ① and ③ in the LH and ② in the RH and note: **After each catch, keep that hand at that position until it makes a throw.**

1. LH tosses ① up at the middle (and, on subsequent cycles, catches ③).

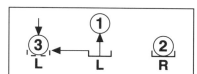

2. RH tosses ② up at the right and catches ①.

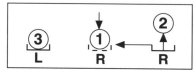

3. LH tosses ③ up at the left, reaches **over** the right arm and catches ②.

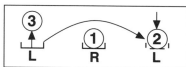

4. RH tosses ① and catches ③.

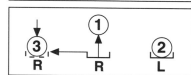

5. LH tosses ② and catches ①.

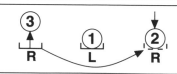

6. RH tosses ③ and catches ②.

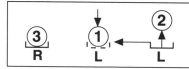

You can now repeat Steps 1-6 for a new cycle of throws and catches.

Now here's something interesting: Notice that at Step 3 the pattern calls for a reach **over** the right arm to catch ②. However, after you have the pattern under control, you might want to give it a bit more vertical symmetry by reaching **under** the right arm on this move. With practice, you will be able to alternate – over, under, over, under, and so on. It's a subtle aesthetic nuance, I admit, and your audience might not even notice the difference, but for stylistic purists, I know that this suggestion will be heartily welcomed as relief from a painful assymetry.

You might also want to reverse the throwing sequence, from **left, middle, right** to **right, middle, left**. To do this, notice that at Step 1 the left hand throws a ball up at the midpoint of the juggle. This makes a symmetrical pattern, with a ball in each hand on either side and one ball high in the middle. This allows you to choose which ball to throw next – left or right. In the pattern outlined above, the **right** hand throws at Step 2. But if instead the **left** hand throws (that would be two left-hand throws in a row), a reversed sequence – right, middle, left – will result.

Here are "reversing" Steps 2 and 3:

Rev. 2. LH (tossing again) tosses ③ up at the left and catches ①.

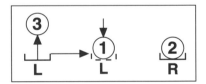

Rev. 3. RH tosses ② up at the right, reaches over (or under) the left arm and catches ③.

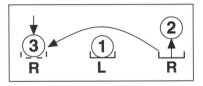

Once begun, the remainder of the reversed sequence moves are so inevitable there's no need to describe them – your hands will know.

* *

Motel for jugglers – The Don't Drop Inn.

* *

Catch under the opposite arm

This "circling" pattern has a lot of Mills' Mess-like charm. It's a bit easier to learn, perhaps, but just as delightfully confusing with its under-the-opposite-arm catches and "backward" tosses – sort of a pseudo-Mess. If you like to perplex, as well as entertain, your friends and fellow jugglers, challenge them with this one.

   Cascade, then...

1. LH, instead of a regular cascade toss, moves over to the right middle of the juggle space and makes a "back- ward" toss of ① to the far left; then, back at left, catches ③ (the ball incoming from the right).

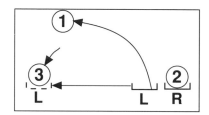

2. RH cascades ②, then reaches **under** the left arm to catch ① and **remains** at the left middle to make its next throw. (NOTE: ① will always be the "backward"-tossed ball.)

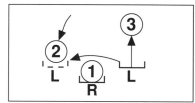

3. LH moves to the right middle of the juggle space and makes a short, straight-up toss of ③, then catches ② at the far left.

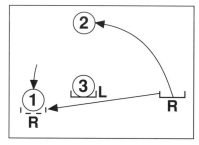

Now we circle the other way:

4. RH makes a "backward" toss of ① from the left middle over to the far right; then catches ③.

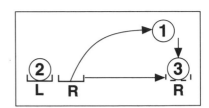

5. LH cascades ②, then reaches under the right arm to catch ① and remains at the right middle to make its next throw.

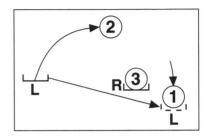

6. RH, moves to the left middle of the juggle space and makes a short straight-up toss of ③, then catches ② at the far right.

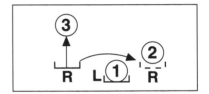

Now repeat Steps 1-6, and so on.

* *

Joe always got together with his juggling buddies
on Thursday night. One Thursday, his wife
suggested they go out to a movie.
"No way, honey," said Joe. "Tonight's my
night out with the balls."

* *

Catch and throw under the opposite arm

In this variation of the Catch Under the Opposite Arm, the left hand begins with the same backward toss of ①, but instead of releasing it from the right **middle**, reaches **under** the right arm and backward-tosses the ball from the **far right side**. Then, when the right hand has caught ① by reaching **under** the left arm, it remains in that **far left** position to start the reverse 3-throw sequence with a backward toss from the far left side.

As a result of these changes, you will see that ① tennises back and forth over the juggle space. Also, the arms cross and recross, and with the intriguing backward tosses and under-the-arm throws and catches, you've got not only an intricate and visually pleasing pattern underway, but one with a very high "baffle" rating.

Start with a Cascade. Then...

1. LH, instead of the usual Cascade toss, reaches **under** the right arm and makes a backward toss of ① over to the far left; then goes left and catches the ball incoming from the right.

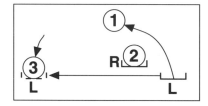

2. RH reverse cascades ②, then reaches **under** the left arm to catch ① and **remains** there to make its next throw from this far left position. Meanwhile, LH, holding ③, drifts over to the **right** middle.

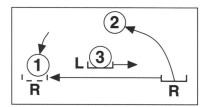

3. LH makes a short toss of ③ straight up; then goes left to catch ② at the left middle.

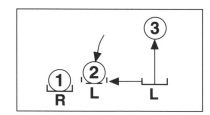

4. RH makes a backward toss of ① from the far left side, from under the left arm over to the far right; then catches ③ at the right middle.

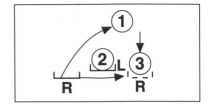

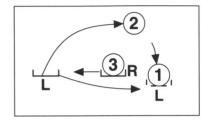

5. LH reverse cascades ②, then reaches under the right arm to catch ① and **remains** there to make its next throw from this far right position. Meanwhile, RH, holding ③, drifts over to the **left** middle.

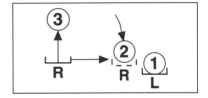

6. RH makes a short toss of ③ straight up; then goes right to catch ② at the right middle.

Now repeat Steps 1-6, and so on.

* *

Juggler: "I think someone's out to get me."
Friend: "What makes you think so?"
Juggler: "I just received a package containing three hand grenades!"

* *

Mills' Mess†

The first time you saw someone doing Mills' Mess, your eyes bugged out, and you knew you had seen your juggling destiny. One day – just as with the four-ball Shower and the five-ball Cascade – one day you would master this mind-boggling pattern of circling balls, crossing and uncrossing hands, and unexpected catches.

Fortunately, Mills' Mess is not the hopelessly confusing puzzle it may seem. A little study, a little practice, some crucial clarifications of the structure of the pattern, and quickly enough you'll begin to sort out the Mess. Yes, it's difficult, but it's **do-able**, so destiny may be closer at hand than you think.

First, some good news – there are only **three** basic throws to learn. These move all three balls, one after the other, first from right to left, then back, from left to right. The count is 1, 2, 3 to the left, 1, 2, 3 to the right.

"Hey!" you're thinking, "This doesn't sound so bad. Tell me more."

Okay. But first, note that I've prefaced my description of Mills' Mess with a two-ball practice juggle that can help you cultivate – at a slower pace – some of the skills you'll need for the three-ball version. However, if you feel confident (and/or impatient) enough, you can skip ahead to page 30 and start right in learning the full Mills' Mess pattern.

TWO-BALL PRACTICE PATTERN

This exercise will help you focus on the unique **toss-catch & carry** that occurs at Step 2 (and again at Step 5) in the three-ball pattern. It's an important key to Mills' Mess success.

Start with a ball in each hand, left arm crossed over right, both hands positioned at the right side of the juggle space. Now make two throws, both from right to left, as follows:

1. LH "back-tosses" ① in a low arc toward the centre of the juggle space then **stays low in the middle** to make the catch described next.

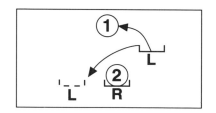

---

†This trick is named after Steve Mills – a three-time IJA champion – who invented and popularised it.

2a. In one continuous movement, RH reverse cascades ②, aiming for the left middle of the juggle space, immediately **catches** ① **at its peak**, and **carries it over the left arm** to the far left.

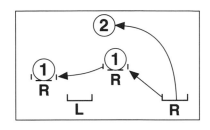

2b. LH, now **under** the right arm, catches ② descending at the left middle.

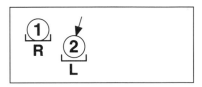

This will help! As you throw ②, **keep your eye on** ① and grab it at its peak.

You'll notice that your arms have reversed their original positions. Both are now at the left side of the juggle space, crossed **right over left**, and ready to toss the balls in the opposite direction as follows:

3. RH "back-tosses" ① in a low arc toward the centre of the juggle and stays low in the middle.

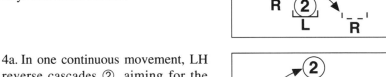

4a. In one continuous movement, LH reverse cascades ②, aiming for the right middle of the juggle space, **catches** ① **at its peak** and **carries it over the right arm** to the far right.

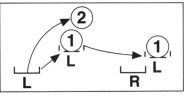

4b. RH, now under the left arm, catches ② descending at the right middle.

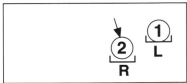

Again, as you throw ②, **keep your eye on** ① and grab it as it peaks.

When this pattern is working smoothly, you'll just need to add one more ball and you'll be doing Mills' Mess! (Don't you love the way some people slip in that word "just"?)

ADDING THE THIRD BALL

When you've got the 2-ball practice pattern under control, you'll be wondering **where** and **when** that third ball enters the pattern. "Right after ②" would be accurate but not a very satisfying answer. Here are the needed details:

To add the third ball, start with the usual Step 1, the familiar back-toss of ①. This time, though, your left hand will also be holding ③, so, after back-tossing ①, **keep your left hand at the right side** and, just after the right hand throws ② (the toss-catch & carry), the left hand will toss ③ **straight up** at the right. Then, exactly as you learned in the 2-ball pattern, the left hand will catch ② at the left middle. (This would be a good time to look at the diagrams for Mills' Mess Steps 1-3.)

Tossing that third ball could be a sticking point, so, as you throw the balls, count "1," "2," and on "3" force yourself to throw that ball **straight up** from **under the right arm**. Until you've got this third throw working, **don't worry about catching anything**.

Now your arms will be in position for the three left- to-right throws, but with this new factor – ③ is in the air at the right. But don't worry; as soon as your right hand back-tosses ① (see Mills' Mess Step 4), it will catch ③ by reflex.

To sum up: When do you throw ③? Right after ②, straight up on the right side. Try it – you have nothing to lose but your composure, your balance, and the friendship of the people downstairs.

MILLS' MESS

Start with two balls in the left hand, one in the right, both held at the right side of the juggle space.

1. LH "back-tosses" ① in a low arc toward the centre of the juggle space (and stays right to make its next toss).

2. RH reverse cascades ②, aiming for the left middle of the juggle space, catches ① at its peak, and carries it over the left arm to the far left.

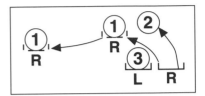

3. LH throws ③ straight up from under the right arm and catches ② at the left middle.

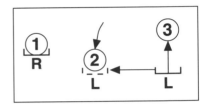

Note that Steps 4, 5, and 6 are simply the mirror image of Steps 1, 2, and 3.

4. RH "back-tosses" ① in a low arc toward the centre of the juggle space, then catches ③ at the right.

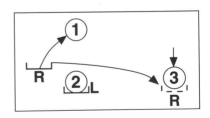

5. LH reverse cascades ②, aiming for the right middle of the juggle space, catches ① at its peak and carries it over the right arm to the far right.

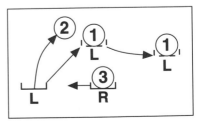

6. RH, at the left, throws ③ straight up from under the left arm and catches ② at the right middle.

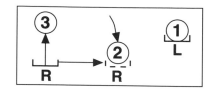

...and so on.

After you master this basic pattern, you'll need to make one small adjustment to perfect the Mess. In Steps 3 and 6, instead of throwing ③ straight up, arc it toward the centre. Then all three balls will be following each other – like little ducks marching over a hill. (Or keep the straight-up throw. It has its own unique charm.)

Chapter 4

Beyond Mills' Mess

Now that you know Mills' Mess, what **else** can be done with it? Well, it can be split in half, turned upside down, split in half while upside down, stretched, as in the "5-count," clawed, performed with back-of-the-hand catches or with altered timing – all of which follow, so tighten your suspenders and get ready for a mess of fun.

Half Mess

Here's a way to produce a shorter, but equally charming, juggle based on the Mills' Mess moves. It uses only one side of the Mills' Mess pattern (Steps 1-4) and – rather than the 1-2-3, 1-2-3 rhythm in the full Mills' Mess – has a 1-2-3-4, 1-2-3-4 count.

Start by doing Steps 1-4 of Mills' Mess (p. 31), but instead of Step 5, do the following move, which is essentially Step 1 repeated, except that the left hand makes its toss at the right middle instead of far right.

Step 1 (repeated): LH tosses ② up from the **right middle** in a slight arc back toward the left, and catches ① at the midpoint.

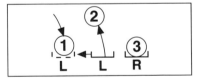

Then continue with Mills' Mess Steps 2, 3, and 4, and so on.

When you've learned the Half Mess, you can increase its excitement by changing the throw in Step 1 to "LH reverse cascades ②" (which will still be the ball that is caught and carried in Step 2).

---

* *

Juggler, passing the hat: "The nicest gift
is something you made yourself…
like money."

---

* *

Inverted Mess

This variation of Mills' Mess begins with the same Mills' Mess move in Step 1 but, at Step 2 the ball is carried **down** and **under**, not **over**, the opposite arm. Hence the term "inverted," though it's used loosely here. The result, of course, is **not** Mills' Mess turned upside down – gravity won't allow that. But the pattern is clearly related to Mills' Mess (the toss-catch & carry at Steps 2 and 5, for instance) and exhibits a lot of the same intriguing complexity.

As with Mills' Mess, the count in this trick is 1-2-3, 1-2-3. And, as a bonus, the Inverted Mess is a good trick to learn as a preparation for The Slam (p. 36), an electrifying move that you'll definitely want to add to your repertoire.

Start with two balls in the left hand, one in the right, with the left hand at the **right middle** of the juggle space…

1. LH tosses ① straight up about 7-8 inches.

2. RH tosses ② in a reverse cascade throw aiming for the middle of the juggle space; then immediately catches ① at its peak and carries it down and to the left.

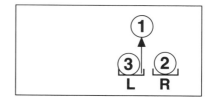

3. LH reverse cascades ③ in a short lob to the right, catches ② and swings back out to the left.

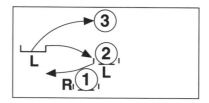

As with the unadulterated Mills' Mess, Steps 4, 5, and 6 are simply the reverse of Steps 1, 2, and 3.

4. RH tosses ① in a short lob straight up about 7-8 inches and goes right to catch ③.

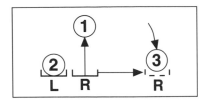

5. LH reverse cascades ② aiming for the middle of the juggle space; then immediately catches ① at its peak and carries it down and to the right.

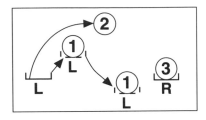

6. RH reverse cascades ③ in a short lob to the left, catches ② and swings back out to the right.

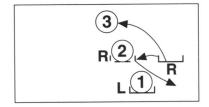

…and so on.

Compare The Inverted Mess and The Slam (p. 36), and you'll find that they are essentially the same. The speed of the slam move is the only difference. Learn either one, and you've got the other.

* *

> They've invented a computer that's so human,
> every so often it goes out in the hallway
> to unwind with a little juggling.

* *

The Slam

In The Slam, instead of the usual Cascade lob, the right hand lifts the ball up to about shoulder height, then throws it across to the left hand on a straight and fast, downward-slanting diagonal. It's a sudden and dramatic move, and you will have to master two tricky catches to perfect it. Here's what you do:
Begin with a Cascade, then...

1. As LH lobs ① to the right just a little bit higher than usual, RH raises ② to shoulder height—getting ready to "slam."

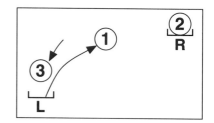

2. RH "slams" ② across to the left hand with a fast, downward-slanting diagonal throw, timing it to pass just over the descending ①, which the RH immediately claw-catches. (To clarify, the RH slam-throw of ② and claw-catch of ① are both part of one continuous arm movement.)

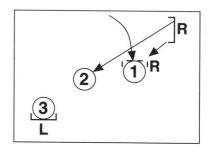

3. Now, barely a nanosecond later, the LH also has a task that requires split-second precision. LH releases ③ in a reverse cascade throw and immediately catches ②, the fast-moving "slam" ball. This accomplished, the Cascade can be resumed.

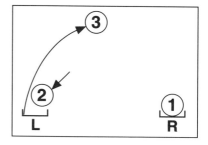

These throws and catches will require practice, but you'll definitely dazzle the crowd with this one, especially when you've mastered the move with **both** hands and can whip off a series of rapid-fire right- and left- hand "slams."

Half of the Inverted Mess

It's possible to do Inverted Mess moves on one side only and produce, not just a variation, but a new juggle that's quite fascinating in its own right. I'll describe the pattern for the right side. Note that the throws and catches are made only at the right, right middle, midpoint, and left middle, which places the juggle essentially on the right side of the juggle space.

Start with two balls in the LH, one in the RH, LH in position at the **right middle**.

1. LH tosses ① straight up about 7-8 inches.

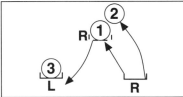

2. RH tosses ② in a reverse cascade throw, aiming for the right middle of the juggle space, then immediately catches ① and carries it down and to the left.

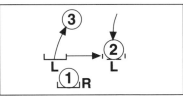

3. LH throws ③ in a short lob from the left middle to the middle, catches ② at the right middle and **stays put** (for a repeat of the throw in Step 1).

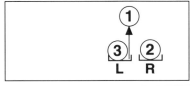

4. RH tosses ① straight up at the left middle (under the left arm) and catches ③ at the midpoint.

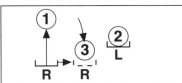

Now the pattern begins to repeat – Step 5 repeating Step 1 with a catch added.

5. LH tosses ② straight up about 7-8 inches, then catches ① descending at the left middle.

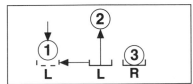

Continue with Steps 2, 3, and 4, and so on.

Gillson's 5-count variation†

In this juggle, which is another variation of the Inverted Mess, you also carry ① **under** the arm – at Steps 2 and 7. You'll also be crossing and uncrossing your arms and making that terrific catch at the midpoint of the juggle that is also one of the highlights of the Mills' Mess pattern.

If you can do both Mills' Mess and the Inverted Mess, you've already acquired most of the motor skills you'll need to do this one. So put them in gear…and go for it!

Start with two balls in the left hand, one in the right, both hands close together at the right side of the juggle space.

1. LH throws ① straight up about 7-8 inches, at the right middle of the juggle space.

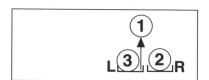

2. RH throws ② straight up at the right, catches ① as it peaks and carries it **under** the left arm.

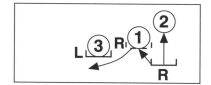

3. LH throws ③ straight up the middle of the juggle, catches ② at the right, reaching over the right arm; **and remains in this position** (until Step 5).

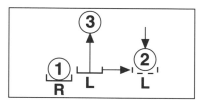

4. RH throws ① straight up at left middle and catches ③ at the midpoint of the juggle.

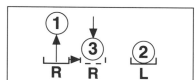

†As for the name – though I discovered this pattern myself, I'm not foolish enough to believe that it has never been done before. Some Neanderthal probably figured it out one lazy Palaeolithic afternoon, fooling around with three marsupial skulls or a trio of baseball-size hunting boulders. Or, it could have been an Egyptian juggler, 5,000 years ago. Or, perhaps, Shirley MacLaine – who knows when? In any case, its origin being conveniently lost in history, I feel free to call it the "Gillson" variation.

5. LH throws ② straight up at the right side of juggle and catches ①.

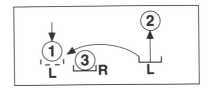

The next five steps are the reverse of the sequence above, and are diagrammed **with new numbers** in case you want to practice beginning with Step 6, in which case you'll hold ① and ③ in your right hand and ② in your left.

---

6. RH throws ① straight up about 7-8 inches, at the left middle of the juggle space (and catches the ball descending at right).

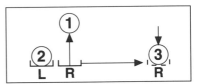

7. LH throws ② straight up at left, catches ① just as it peaks, and carries it **under** the right arm.

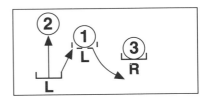

8. RH throws ③ straight up the middle of the juggle, catches ② at the left, reaching **over** the left arm, **and remains in this position** (until Step 10).

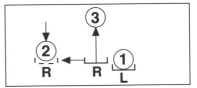

9. LH throws ① straight up at right middle and catches ③ at the midpoint of the juggle.

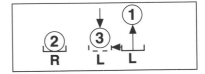

10. RH throws ② straight up at left side of the juggle and catches ①.

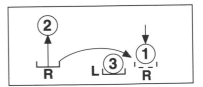

Mills' simultaneous

This is a small, close, fast and furious juggle. It begins with the first two steps of the Mills' Mess pattern, but at Step 3, two balls are tossed up simultaneously from the crossed-arms position, and after that, every other throw is a two-ball simultaneous throw with the **arms crossed** – first right over left, then left over right. It's speedy and almost impossible to decipher when you see it performed, but take it a step at a time and you'll soon be showing off a dynamite little baffler, something like a miniature explosion in a ball factory.

As with the regular Mills' Mess, start with two balls in the left hand and one in the right, hands next to each other at the **right** side of the juggle space.

1. LH throws ① from the right side straight up about 5 inches.

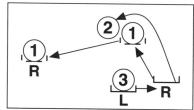

2. RH tosses ② with a reverse cascade throw, aiming for the midpoint of the juggle space, then immediately catches ① at its peak and carries it to the left over the left arm.

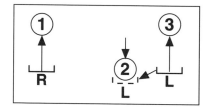

3. LH and RH, now in a crossed-arms position—right over left—simultaneously toss ① and ③ straight up about 7-8 inches. Then LH catches ② at the juggle midpoint.

* *

How do you learn to juggle?
…drop by drop!

* *

4. LH, carrying quickly to the left side, tosses ② in a reverse cascade throw, aiming for the midpoint of the juggle space. Then, simultaneously, as they peak, LH claws ① and RH, having moved to the right side, claws ③, after which the arms are again crossed, this time **left over right** to go smoothly into the next simultaneous tosses.

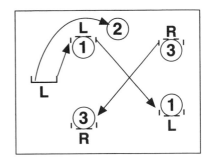

5. LH and RH toss ① and ③, respectively, straight up about 7-8 inches. This time RH catches ② at the juggle midpoint.

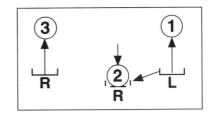

6. RH, carrying quickly to the right side, tosses ② in a reverse cascade throw, aiming for the midpoint of the juggle space. Then simultaneously, as they peak, RH claws ① and LH claws ③ and the arms are crossed again, **right over left**, in readiness for the next simultaneous tosses.

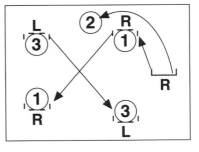

Now go back to – and then cycle and recycle – Steps 3, 4, 5, and 6.

Above and beyond Mills' Mess

Some people like to reach for the moon – some need to go **even furthe**r! So, reach for the moon – try Mills' Mess and **claw** every throw and catch. The result is a juggle admirable for both its beauty and its difficulty.

And beyond that – a move almost bizarre in its difficulty (and I've seen someone do it) – the Mills' Mess pattern with all throws and catches made on the backs of the hands, fork-style! Now that's shooting for the stars! (There are several more conventional "fork" juggles in Chapter 6).

Chapter 5

Showers and
2-in-1-Hand Tricks

Someone has defined juggling as keeping in the air more objects than the number of hands doing the throwing. Thus juggling would be two objects kept aloft with one hand, or three objects kept aloft with two hands, or four objects kept…well, I suppose the definition sort of peters out here, but assuming we need a definition at all, the above seems good enough. And it follows, therefore, that the 2-in-1-Hand – being the **simplest** form of juggling – must have been the first, the **original**, juggle.

How and when did this happen? Let's go back a few million years and indulge in some imaginative history. Picture, if you will, a caveman – finally erect on two legs, hands free for whatever purpose, and, in fact, one primary purpose was to pitch rocks at whatever dangerous (or perhaps tasty) animal was around. In those days of snakes, bears, tigers, and the like behind every tree or bush, you didn't want to go anywhere without a rock in your hand, or, if you were smart, **two** rocks.

So, one sunny afternoon, our hero (incidentally, a beautifully coordinated guy, despite having a name that sounded like a grunt) was holding two rounded hunting boulders in his RH. It's not far-fetched to suppose that, in an idle moment, he tossed one of the boulders into the air, as he had done many times before. This time, though, in a burst of inspiration, as the first boulder was peaking, he tossed up the second boulder and caught the first! I don't think it matters whether he actually caught the second boulder, for at that moment, in the warm sunlight of that primitive landscape, Fate had placed the mantle of greatness across his hairy shoulders. Imagine! Was he not holding in his hand the very **Adam** of juggling balls – Old Number ① himself?

Almost certainly, then, the 2-in-1-Hand was the first juggle. And it, quite naturally, would have led to a 3-rock Shower pattern. Only much later would the Cascade appear. It would have taken a prehistoric Einstein to simply pick up **three** boulders and swing into a 3-Ball Cascade! No way.

In any case, good luck with the 2-in-1-Hand juggles and the sprinkling of Showers that follow. And may you add glory to this ancient skill.

Statue of Liberty

Hold your left hand up (in a comfortable position) just like the Lady in the Harbour. Now, one after the other, float each ball up from the right hand to a point about 2-3 inches above the upraised left, so that the ball settles into the left hand just after the left hand does a gravity-drop of the preceding ball down into the right hand. Technically, it's a Shower (circular) pattern with one ball flying up, one in the upstretched hand about to fall, and one gravity-dropping. For best results, keep the left arm as immobile as possible (and you might want to wear a pale green shirt).

As with any Shower pattern, it will be easier to learn this trick if you practice it with one ball and then with two before trying it with all three balls.

Start with two balls in the right hand, one in the up- stretched left hand.

1. RH floats ① up 2-3 inches above the LH.

2. LH gravity drops ②, catches ①.

3. RH tosses ③ up, catches ②.

…and so on.

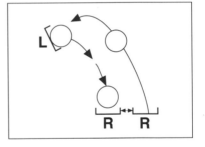

(NOTE: The diagram shows the ongoing juggle. As is true of all Shower patterns, each ball follows the exact same path, so it would be redundant to include a separate – virtually identical – diagram for each step.)

Statue of Liberty variation

Hold the left hand high as you do in the Statue of Liberty, **but** keep a slight bend in the elbow. Then, instead of the usual gravity-drops from the left hand, send each ball, with a pumping motion, **up and over** the next incoming ball. Try to make each throw from the right hand float precisely up to the level of the left hand – no higher. Then, just before it arrives, pump the left hand throw over it. If you choose, you can make these left hand throws **very high and wide**. It then becomes a giant juggle!

High Half Shower

To explain the name – "shower" means that every ball travels the same "circular" path (here, a sort of rounded rectangle), as in the conventional shower pattern; "high" means that the right hand remains upraised, making each catch, short carry, and release at head level; and "half" tells us that the right hand releases each ball with a short upward lob, as in the conventional Half Shower. The lob slows things down a bit and makes this a rather leisurely juggle. Try it; there are only two throws to learn.

Start with a cascade, then...

1. LH throws ① **under** the right arm, straight up the **right** side of the juggle space to a point about head high, then catches the ball descending at the left.

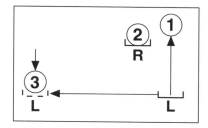

2. RH, holding ② **palm up** at head level, carries it 10-12 inches to the left, lobs it a few inches straight up, then moves 10-12 inches back to the right for a high catch of ①.

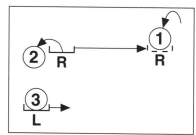

Now just keep alternating Steps 1 and 2.

The See Saw

In this pattern, the ball on the right side of the juggle goes straight up as the one on the left comes straight down. Then, the left goes up as the right comes down, and so on, in a continuous see-saw fashion. What about the third ball? It gets zipped back and forth on a horizontal path between the two hands, thrown **simultaneously** with **each** straight-up toss from either hand. Thus you're always **throwing** two balls at once (one straight up and the other across) and **catching** two balls at once. So get ready – it may be called the See Saw, but it's not child's play!

RH holds two balls, LH holds one.

1. RH tosses ① up about 18 inches.

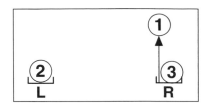

2. LH tosses ② straight up (same height as ①). **Simultaneously**, RH zips ③ straight across for a LH catch, then catches ①.

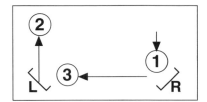

3. RH tosses ① straight up. **Simultaneously**, LH zips ③ straight across for a RH catch, then catches ②.

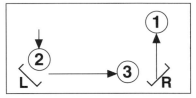

Now repeat Steps 2 and 3 as often as you wish.

When you've mastered the pattern, you'll discover that from The See Saw you can move smoothly into either a clockwise or counter-clockwise Shower, and, conversely, switch from a Shower into a See Saw pattern.

SEE SAW VARIATION

As I've warned, The See Saw will take a bit of practice to learn. But once you've got it, the following intriguing variation should come fairly easily.

Do Steps 1 and 2 of The See Saw – the right hand tosses ① straight up, the left hand tosses ② straight up, and the right hand zips ③ across (the zip move). Now stall for one beat – that is, instead of the zip move, the left hand tosses ③ straight up just to the left of the descending ②, which it then catches (a simple 2-in-1-Hand exchange). **Then** do Step 3 – the right hand tosses ① straight up and the left zips ② across and catches ③.

Then stall again for one beat – the right hand tosses ② straight up just to the right of the descending ①, which it then catches. **Then** ① across to the left and catches ②...and so on.

Briefly, it's toss and zip across, 2-in-1-Hand, toss and zip the other way, 2-in-1-Hand, etc.

The 4-4-1

This more advanced variation of the See Saw is named for its throws – 4 being the height of a throw in a typical 4-ball juggle – about 18" – and 1 being a straight across "zip". Thus...

RH holds two balls, ① and ③; LH holds one, ②; and, to a 1-2-3 count, RH tosses ① straight up; then LH tosses ② straight up; then RH zips ③ to LH (and catches ①).

That's one sequence, now the reverse. LH tosses ③ straight up (outside falling ②, which it catches). RH tosses ① straight up; LH zips ② across to RH. That's the second sequence; now repeat both to continue.

The Double Box

Some jugglers, focusing on the **shape** of the pattern rather than the **see-sawing** effect, call The See Saw "The Box". And since in the following variation we create two side-by-side boxes, we can call this trick The Double Box. I suppose it could be called the "Double See Saw," but then, what's in a name? As Shakespeare put it, **in a direct reference to juggling** (unfortunately, almost always misquoted), "Th'rows by any other name..." LH tosses ③ straight up and RH zips.

But seriously, hold two balls in the RH, one in the LH. Then...

1. RH tosses ① straight up about 18 inches.

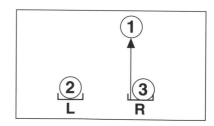

2. LH tosses ② straight up the same height as ①. **Simultaneously**, RH zips ③ straight across to LH. LH catches ③; RH catches ①.

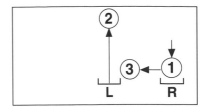

Now quickly shift both hands to the left the width of the first "box." The RH is now where the LH was – in position to catch the descending ②. Then repeat exactly the moves in Step 2. That is…

3. LH tosses ③ straight up. **Simultaneously**, RH zips ① straight across to LH. LH catches ①; RH catches ②.

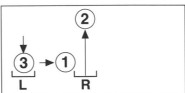

4. RH tosses ② straight up. **Simultaneously**, LH zips ① straight across to RH. RH catches ①; LH catches ③.

Now shift both hands **back to their original position** and repeat exactly the moves in Step 4. That is…

5. RH tosses ① straight up. **Simultaneously**, LH zips ③ straight across to RH. RH catches ③; LH catches ②.

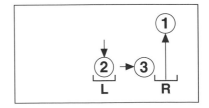

Continue by repeating Steps 2-5 as often as you like.

* *

Anyone can juggle if they have the balls.

* *

See Saw Slam

The basic See Saw pattern is U-shaped—two balls travel vertically up and down at the sides while the third ball zips back and forth in short horizontal throws across the middle. To do the "Slam" variation, we simply shift a ball from its column on the right side to move up and down a column in the centre of the juggle space. Now a high-speed horizontal "Slam" throw will pass, right to left, over the centre ball as it falls, and then back over it, left to right, on the return throw just before the centre ball is tossed up the column again. When it's working nicely, the ball in the centre column will seem to be mysteriously appearing from out of nowhere.

Hold two balls in the right hand, one in the left...

1. RH tosses ① straight up the middle of the juggle space.

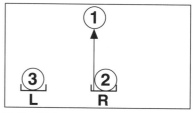

2. RH then moves to the right and delivers ② in a carefully timed, speedy, horizontal throw across to the LH **over**, and a split-second later, catches, the descending ①.

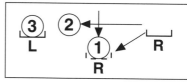

3. LH throws ③ straight up and catches ② (like in the See Saw).

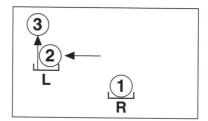

4. LH zips ② back across to the right (a return "Slam"), passing the ball **over** ① held in the RH.

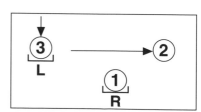

5. RH tosses ① straight up the centre column **after** ② has crossed over, then quickly catches ② at the right.

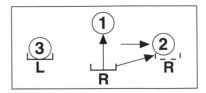

Then repeat Steps 2-5, and so on.

Editor's Note: After working on this trick for several hours, I zipped a memo off to George, asking, "Is this **possible**? I can't keep ① under control **and** catch ② in Step 5." His reply: "Keep trying! I can do it and I've seen others do it (it looks terrific!), and I'm sure it's accurate as written. Try using a **slow** "slam" throw at first, and notice that the RH moves are like those in Centering 2 and 3 [p. 62]."

Two Hand High Catch

At some point, while doing a 3-ball, side-by-side columns pattern, with a lone "centre" ball and two "outside" balls, you throw the outside balls up twice as high as usual then reach way up and claw-catch them as they peak.

To get the timing for this catch, count "1" as you toss up the centre ball and "2" as you toss up the two outside balls. Practice this cadence for a minute— "1-2, 1-2, 1-2," then, just after you say "2" and the outside balls reach their peak, in one movement, you say "1," throw up the centre ball, and claw-catch the two outside balls. (You might not have any timing troubles, but if you do, the cadence tactic should help.)

Suggestion: As a natural follow-up to the high catches described above, you can claw the balls down, **cross them** under the centre ball and then throw them straight up in the two outside columns.

Alternating Columns Carries

I'm sure you've seen someone do a columns juggle and then begin to **carry** one of the "outside" balls up and down instead of **tossing** it. It always gets a laugh— the lazy juggler! "Look! Nothing's happening!"

We shall now see that by a simple switching manoeuvre this carry can be done first on one side, then on the other, and, if you wish, back and forth repeatedly. This expansion of the trick is sure to add to the fun, and it transforms the joke into a bit of bona fide juggling magic!

1. Do a three columns juggle with LH juggling ① and ② side by side and RH raising and lowering ③ by hand.

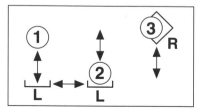

2. When LH has just tossed ② up the centre column and caught ① at the left, and RH has lowered hand-held ③, the juggle is symmetrical—a ball in each hand and one aloft in the centre. Therefore you have an option to go either way—RH can **carry** ③ up again and LH simultaneously **toss** ① (and catch ②), or you can do the reverse – Step 3.

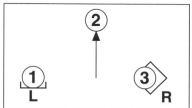

3. LH **carries** ① up and, simultaneously, RH **tosses** ③, then catches ②.

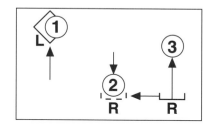

When you've taught yourself the switch from right to left, try switching back, left to right. Then try switching back and forth on **every** throw of the pair ① and ③. This switching skill will come in handy when you try The Weave (p. 60) and The Double String (p. 55).

Three Balls Arcing

If you can do a 2-in-1-Hand juggle and keep the third ball going up and down in tandem with the other "outside" ball, then you're ready to learn Three Balls Arcing.

I was tempted to name the trick The Rainbow, but, in fact, the resemblance is not so strong. Of course, a convincing rainbow effect could be created if I tried it with six balls coloured red, orange, yellow, green, blue, and violet. In fact, I've make a terrific start already…I bought the coloured balls.

But back to reality and the possible…

RH holds ① and ③. LH holds ②.

1. RH throws ① in a low arc toward the left hand.

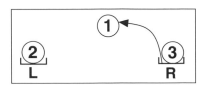

2. As ① peaks, both hands simultaneously throw ② and ③ so that they cross over in two higher arcs, making sure that ② describes the middle arc, travelling left to right, and ③ describes the highest arc, right to left. Then LH catches ①.

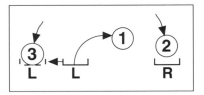

3. As ② and ③ peak, LH tosses ① back to the right along the same low arc. Then ② and ③ are caught.

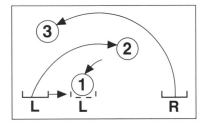

4. As ① peaks, ② and ③ are simultaneously thrown crossover again, ② once more tracing the middle arc and ③ the high arc. Then RH catches ①.

…and so on.

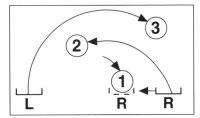

The Follow

The Follow is a variation on The Exchange (page 57) and, like that pattern, uses a 2-in-1-hand juggle with an exchange ("new" ball in, "old" ball out) made on **every other** toss. In The Follow, the right hand is kept low as it performs a 2-in-1-hand juggle. The left hand brings a "new" ball over in a wide clockwise arc and, on its downswing, "follows" a ball that is dropping into the right hand. This neatly timed follow is the principal effect of the pattern.

To do The Follow, just follow the following:

With RH, do a low 2-in-1-Hand clockwise juggle. LH holds the third ball.

1. RH, instead of the usual 2-in-1-Hand clockwise throw, lobs ① straight up at the **left middle**. **At the same moment,** LH (palm up) swings in a wide clockwise arc, carrying ② over ① and following ③ straight down toward RH. LH stops (with ② in it) 5-6 inches above RH at the exact moment that ③ plops into RH.

2. LH now lobs ② straight up about 4-5 inches and quickly reaches over to catch ①. (This movement leftward is the beginning of the next circular swing.)

3. RH tosses ③ up in a regular 2-in-1-Hand clockwise throw and catches ②.

Now repeat the 3-step sequence.

NOTE: ① and ② are continually exchanged, but ③ never leaves the 2-in-1-Hand pattern. Furthermore, ③ is always the ball that you follow as it drops into the right hand.

* *

A juggler's income?
Last year I was in the Fortune 500.
I was one of the zeros.

* *

The Follow – both sides

Most one-sided juggles can be expanded to create a "both-sides" pattern, and The Follow illustrates this idea very well.

First, learn to do The Follow competently on **either** side. Then, with a few slight adjustments (for instance, the rhythm changes from 1-2-3, 1-2-3 to 1-2, 1-2), you'll be ready to perform the steps described below.

As with The Follow, start with a 2-in-1-Hand juggle with ① and ③ in the right hand and the left hand holding ②.

1. RH, instead of the usual 2-in-1-Hand clockwise throw, moves to the left and lobs ① straight up at the left middle. **At the same moment**, LH (palm up) swings over in a clockwise arc, carrying ② over ① and following ③ straight down toward the RH. LH stops (with ② in it) 5-6 inches above RH at the exact moment that ③ plops into RH.

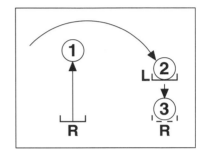

2. LH "back-tosses" ② over to the left, then catches ① at the left middle.

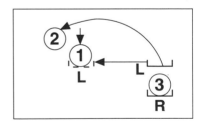

3. LH moves to the right and tosses ① straight up at the right middle (that's two LH tosses in a row), then catches ② descending at the left. **At the same moment**, RH (palm up) swings over in a counterclockwise arc, carrying ③ over ① and following ② straight down toward the LH, stopping just over it as LH catches ②.

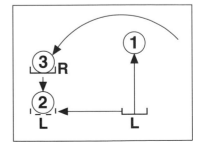

4. RH "back-tosses" ③ over to the right, then catches ① at the right middle.

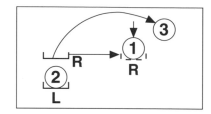

Repeat Steps 1-4, and so on.

Giant Follow

Try this Follow – Both Sides variation. Make enormous circles with left arm extended full-length in Step 1 and right arm likewise extended in Step 3. It should be a large and leisurely pattern, so always throw ① about a foot and a half high to slow the pace. Its giant size transforms the pattern into a whole new trick.

* *

Ball A looks like B
And Ball B looks like C
And Ball C looks a lot
    like their brother;
So how d'ya unravel
The paths that they travel
When you can't tell the
    one from the other?

* *

The String

Almost certainly, you have seen The String (also called The Yo-Yo). Two balls are juggled side-by-side in a 2-in-1-Hand pattern while the third ball – hand-held a few inches above one of them – moves up and down and seems to raise and lower it by means of an invisible string. It's a pleasing and powerful illusion and an absolute must for every juggler.

To perform The String, do a side-by-side 2-in-1-Hand pattern with your left hand. With your right hand, hold the third ball about 4 or 5 inches over the ball on the right side of the pattern, moving it up and down always at the same distance above the ball as it rises and falls.

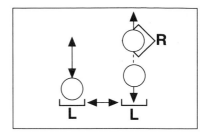

Once you've mastered The String with your right hand, learn the trick with your left. Then you'll be ready to learn the two String variations that follow.

Double String

In the Double String, you perform The String effect, first on the right side of the juggle, then smoothly switch it over to the left side. Thusly...

1. Do The String with the RH raising and lowering ①, the upper ball of the "connected" pair. Notice that as you lower The String, the bottom "dangling" ball—②—drops back into the LH (which has just tossed ③ up the left-side column). At this moment, you are holding a ball in each hand – RH above LH.

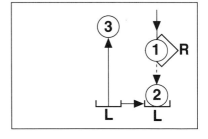

2. As ③ peaks, swing ① and ② under it in a U-shaped arc and come up on the other side, left over right. As you go up, LH holds on to ② and RH tosses up ① beneath it, creating The String effect on the left side of the juggle pattern. Then RH catches ③.

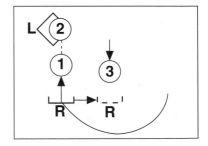

By using this "swing-under" move and then reversing it, you can switch The String from side to side as often as you like.

Around the String

This fascinating manoeuvre is one of my favourites. Learn it, and you'll see why. It embellishes, and enhances, the basic String effect by sending one ball flying in a circle around the String-connected pair. The combined effect of The String plus the circumjected† third ball is levitational magic!

1. Do The String and as RH raises ① (the upper ball of the String-connected pair) LH tosses ② up to follow it and catches ③.

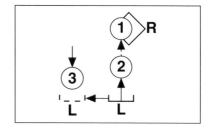

2. LH reaches under right arm and throws ③ up the **right** side of the pattern in a counterclockwise, looping arc that travels over the String and will descend on the left side of the pattern. LH then catches ②.

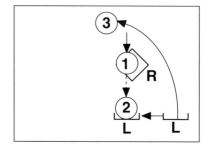

Repeat Steps 1 and 2 as many times as you like.

Once you've got this looping circular throw around The String mastered, you might also try throwing ③ in the reverse, clockwise direction. Or, the left hand can throw ③ clockwise over The String, catch it on the far right and immediately send it back over in the reverse direction!

---

†"Circumjected" is a word of my own coining – I needed a word for "thrown in a circle", a situation probably unique to juggling (and perhaps wrestling).

Elbow Fake

While cascading, bring your left arm over and from just in front of your right elbow, throw a ball from the left hand straight up in the air and simultaneously, snap the elbow up as if you were bouncing the ball off it. This can be done just once, or repeated many times, using a 2-in-1-Hand juggle in the left hand and keeping that hand near the right elbow, which you snap up with every throw.

The Exchange (or The "Drop")

As the left hand does a counterclockwise 2-in-1-Hand juggle, the right hand, held shoulder high, drops a "new" ball into the juggle and immediately removes an ascending "old" ball – that's The Exchange. This manoeuvre can be performed once, or continuously, where **every other ball** tossed up in the 2-in-1-Hand juggle is removed and a new ball dropped in. When performed crisply and smoothly, this juggle has a nice "machine" or "robot" look.

1. LH tosses ① **straight** up the middle (not counterclockwise this time) and catches the ball descending at left. RH, meanwhile, is bringing ② over ① as it rises.

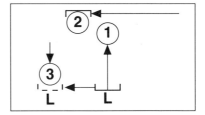

2a. Now a drop and a throw happen simultaneously. RH drops ② down the left-hand column, then claw catches ① at its peak and carries it straight out to the right about 12-15 inches.

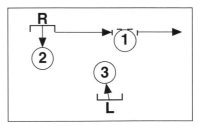

2b. Simultaneously, LH tosses ③ up **counterclockwise** at the centre and it peaks just as RH reaches its rightmost position. (There is no exchange on this throw.) LH then catches ②.

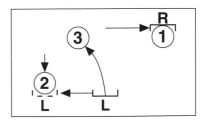

For a continuous juggle, keep alternating Step 1 (LH toss straight up) and Step 2 (RH exchange (Step 2a.) and LH counterclockwise throw (Step 2b.) performed simultaneously).

Now for a terrific variation: Instead of bringing the ball straight across the front of your body for the "drop," swing it around behind your head and over your shoulder to reach the same drop-off point. Sounds and looks **very** difficult, but, in fact, is only **somewhat** difficult. Also, learn The Exchange with the **left hand** doing the "drop." Then try the around-the-head manoeuvre with that hand. Eventually (well before the year 2000), you'll be able to swing the ball around behind your head for a drop in front, in **both** directions – that is, making alternate left- and right-side drops.

One last challenge – The Exchange **can** be performed on **every** throw. Hold your right hand a little higher and move it back and forth only about 8-10 inches between the catch and the drop. This transforms The Exchange into a very fast (and very challenging) upside-down Shower pattern.

Slam Exchange

In essence (and even in Seattle), the Slam Exchange is a 2-in-1-Hand pattern in side-by-side columns – here performed with the left hand. ③ simply travels straight up and down in the left-side column throughout. The slam and exchange occur every time that ③ goes up. At that moment, the right hand fires the ball it is holding in a fast, diagonally downward "slam" to the left hand, and immediately catches the ball tossed just before (the "exchange"), which is then peaking in the right-side column.

Step 1 is a starting move – to make the moves easier to learn. Steps 2 and 3 are the pattern itself.

Hold two balls in the left hand, one in the right.

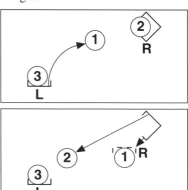

1. LH lobs ①, aiming it a bit rightward so as to peak at the centre of the juggle space, where it will be caught. Meanwhile, RH is raised up preparing for a "slam."

2a. RH slams ②, over ①, and immediately claw-catches ① as part of the same movement.

2b. As RH "slams," LH tosses ③ straight up, then catches the "slam" ball, ②.

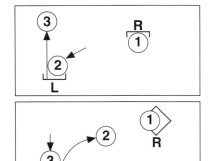

3. LH lobs ②, aiming it to peak at the centre of the juggle space, then catches ③.

Continue repeating Steps 2 and 3.

2-in-1-Hand Tennis

Like the basic patterns in Chapter 1, this is a relatively simple trick that is nevertheless fascinating and fun in its own right. And, like those patterns, it also leads to some terrific variations, as you shall see when you advance to Cross-Arm Tennis (p. 65), Burke's Barrage (p. 66) and Rubenstein's Revenge (p. 68).

Never having encountered any "official" name, and despite the fact that three balls are used, I call it 2-in-1-Hand Tennis because each hand takes a turn doing a brief 2-in-1-Hand juggle, while the third ball goes back and forth as in a tennis game. Try it and you'll see that the name does fit.

Start with two balls in the left hand, one in the right.

1. LH, with a reverse cascade throw, tosses ① over toward the right hand. (Next time around, LH will catch ③.)

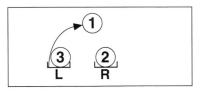

2. RH tosses ② straight up just to the **left** of ① as it crosses over, and catches ①.

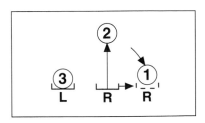

3. RH, again, with a reverse cascade throw, tosses ① back toward the left and catches ②.

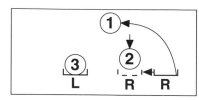

4. LH tosses ③ straight up and just to the **right** of ① as it crosses over, and catches ①.

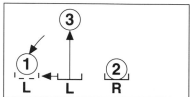

Repeat Steps 1-4.

To clarify a bit, ② and ③ always go straight up and down and always remain in the same hand. ① "tennises" back and forth between the two hands. Also, each hand makes two consecutive throws, so the ongoing rhythm is L-R-R-L-L-R-R-L-L and so on.

When this basic manoeuvre feels comfortable, you'll be ready for the variations on it later in this chapter.

Two-Hand Weave

First with one hand, then the other, alternating from side to side, you carry a ball in S-shaped paths through the spaces that momentarily open in a 2-in-1-Hand juggle. The passes create a symmetrical, snake-like weaving pattern. A languid flute accompaniment, if it can be arranged, will add to the mood of writhing, exotic sensuality.

Hold ① and ② in the right hand and ③ in the left and begin a 2-in-1-Hand clockwise juggle using ① and ②.

1. Just as RH begins to throw ① up (clockwise) at the centre (this will feel like a RH throw under the left arm), LH carries ③ **over** ①, down, and then horizontally straight out to the left **underneath** ① as it rises. As you make this looping carry, ② will drop into your RH.

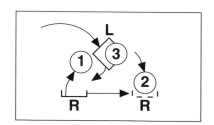

2. RH throws ② up slightly counter-clockwise at the centre (this is the switch over to a **LH** 2-in-1-Hand juggle) and catches ①. Meanwhile, completing a reversed S-shaped path, LH carries ③ back toward the centre for its next throw.

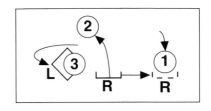

3. Just as LH begins to throw ③ up (slightly counterclockwise) at the centre, (feels like a LH throw under the right arm), RH carries ① over ③, down, and then horizontally out to the right underneath ③ as it rises. As you make this carry, ② will drop into your LH.

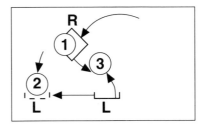

4. LH tosses ② up slightly clockwise at the centre (this is the switch over to a RH 2-in-1-Hand juggle) and catches ③. Meanwhile, completing an S-shaped path, RH carries ① back in toward the centre for its next throw.

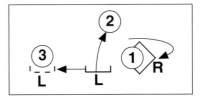

Repeat Steps 1-4.

Here's the path that the carried balls travel through the pattern.

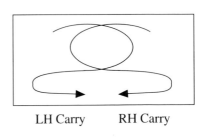

LH Carry   RH Carry

* *

The secret method of the great Chinese jugglers?
T'ai Ming.

* *

Centering 2 and 3

When you've mastered the 2-in-1-Hand Tennis juggle, make this slight adjustment. Instead of tossing ② and ③ up at the right and left sides, throw each **straight up the centre** of the juggle space, while tennising ① back and forth as before. When these new centre throws feel comfortable, add the following flourishes.

CARRIES BEHIND THE BACK

1. As soon as RH tennises ① and catches ③ descending in the centre, carry ③ around behind your back. (In subsequent sequences, LH will carry ② from behind the back around to the front for the centre toss in Step 2.)

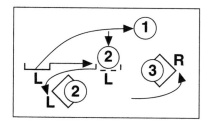

2. LH throws ② up at the centre and ③ should reach your backbone just as LH catches ① at the left.

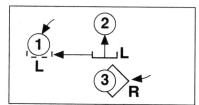

3. LH tennises ① to the right, catches ② dropping at the centre and swings it around behind the back.

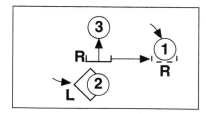

4. RH carries ③ around to the front, makes a centre toss and catches ① just as ② reaches your backbone.

Back to Step 1…and so on.

Notice that in Carries Behind the Back and in the following variation one hand "works," that is, makes two consecutive throws, while the other is "idle". Perhaps you can invent some additional interesting motions for the "idle" hand to perform.

TOUCH THE BALL TO THE BODY

Juggle, centering ② and ③, as above, but instead of carries behind the back, bring each ball, in turn, up to touch the top of the head, or the ear – like a telephone. Both this and the Carries Behind the Back juggle yield a mysterious, and humourous, "connected-by-strings" effect as the balls rise up. You'll get laughs! Want more fun? Juggle as before, but now carry ② and ③ alternately straight down to touch the thighs. A nice marching robot look is achieved. Nice, that is, if you like marching robots.

* *

I learned incredible control of the hands from my uncle.
He worked the night shift in a dairy,
had to milk the cows without waking them up.

* *

2-in-1-Hand Shower

Why this name for a 3-ball pattern? Because it contains elements of both the 2-in-1-Hand and the Shower patterns. It starts with a 2-in-1-Hand juggle, then Shower throws are interspersed. I considered calling it "The 2-in-1-Hand with Interspersed Showers," but it would have sounded like a weather report instead of a juggle.

Start with a "columns" juggle – that is, ① comes down the centre column as ② and ③ go straight up on either side synchronously. RH catches ① and then...

1. LH showers ② (over ①) to the right and, at the same instant, RH **zips** ③ straight across to the LH (under ①) and then catches ①. (The 2-in-1-Hand **See Saw** Shower?)

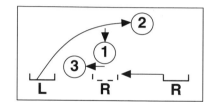

2. RH cascades ① to the left and catches ②. (I think I've got it now – The 2-in-1-Hand See Saw Shower **Cascade**!)

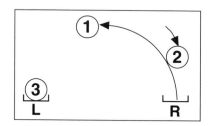

3. RH showers ② to the left and, simultaneously, LH zips ③ across to the RH and catches ①.

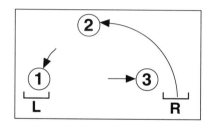

4. LH cascades ① to the right and catches ②.

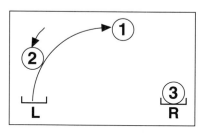

Now repeat the 4-step sequence, and note: ① is always cascaded; ③ is always the "zipped" ball; and ② **tennises** (!) back and forth. So there you have it – "The 2-in-1-Hand See Saw **Tennis** Shower Cascade!"

* *

Juggling is a sym-ball-ic activity.

* *

Cross-arm Tennis

In this variation of 2-in-1-Hand Tennis, you "tennis" one ball back and forth between the left and right hands just as you do in the basic trick, but now the right hand will make its straight-up toss and catch on the **left** side, and the left hand will toss and catch on the **right** side. The result is a pattern that is not only a spell-binder in its own right but **also** gives you the essential pattern that underlies the two complicated and very classy juggles that complete this chapter—Burke's Barrage and Rubenstein's Revenge.

Start with two balls in the right hand, one in the left.

1. RH tosses ① straight up on the right side. (This is a starting move only.)

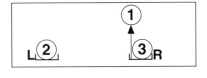

2. LH reverse cascades ② (the "tennis" ball) to the right and claws down ① on the **right**. The right arm moves **leftward** as the left arm crosses **over** it.

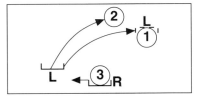

Now come two consecutive RH throws.

3. RH tosses ③ straight up underneath the left arm on the **left** side, then goes right to catch ②.

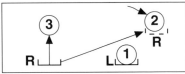

4. RH reverse cascades ② to the left and claws down ③ on the left, crossing **over** the left arm.

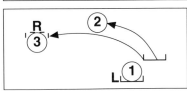

Now come two consecutive LH throws (Step 5 and then Step 2 repeated).

5. LH tosses ① straight up underneath the right arm on the right side, then goes left to catch ②.

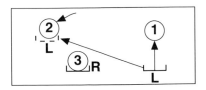

Now repeat Steps 2-5.

Burke's Barrage

Although Burke's Barrage (named after its inventor, Ken Burke) derives from the Cross-Arm Tennis pattern, it's about ten times more active, and you might have trouble spotting the family resemblance. Both arms are constantly in motion, crossing the body, throwing, catching and carrying, like windmills flailing in a storm. But, surprisingly, Burke's Barrage simply adds flourishes – elaborate, wheel-like carries – to the Cross-Arm Tennis pattern, executed, one on each side, by the arm that is "idle" (as defined on p. 63). The resulting "Barrage" is no misnomer – when you see the trick performed, those wheeling carries really come atcha! No question that in Burke's Barrage we have, as my friend Noah put it, "One of the major 3-ball moves."

Start with two balls in the right hand, one in the left.

1. RH tosses ① straight up about shoulder height at the **right** side of the juggle space. (NOTE: This is a starting move only. Henceforth only LH will throw and catch ①, just as only RH will throw and catch ③.)

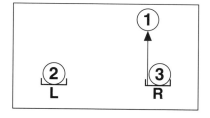

2. LH "tennises" ② in a short arc over to the right. (② will tennis back and forth throughout.) Then LH claw-catches ① and carries it down and around through more than a full counterclockwise circle on the **right** side of the body. The "wheel" it describes should point more or less forward like the right wheel on a car. (This carry will terminate with the LH throw to be described in Step 5.) While this is happening, RH will make the two consecutive throws described next.

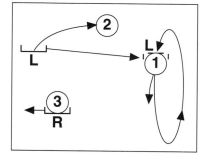

3. RH tosses ③ straight up about shoulder height, at the **left** side of the juggle space and **under the left arm** as that arm wheels through the back part of its counterclockwise carry. Then RH catches ② at the right.

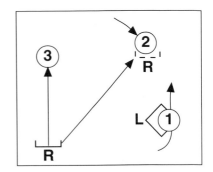

4. RH tennises ② in a short arc over to the left. Then RH claw-catches ③ and carries it down and around through more than a full clockwise "wheel" on the **left** side of the body. (The carry will end with a repeat of the RH throw in Step 3, but only after LH has made its two consecutive throws described next.)

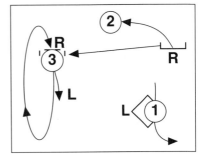

5. LH tosses ① straight up about shoulder height, at the **right** side of the juggle space and **under the right arm** as that arm wheels through the back part of its clockwise circular carry. LH then catches ② at the left.

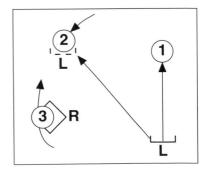

The left hand throws again (an exact repeat of Step 2), and from this point on the juggle continues with each hand making **two consecutive throws** while the other is busy making its long "wheel" carry.

Rubenstein's Revenge†

I saw someone doing it – an unbelievable whirling and twirling, crossing and uncrossing of arms, and it took me almost a month – not to **learn** it – but just to figure out what in the name of blazing beanbags it was that I'd seen! Fortunately, I was already familiar with both Burke's Barrage and The Weave, so I was able to spot the similar elements and gradually piece together what the pattern had to be.

Surprisingly, despite the continuous activity described below – **both** arms making broad circular carries in **both clockwise and counterclockwise** directions – the Revenge gives the appearance of a **leisurely** (!?) juggle with the gratifying feeling of an inevitable logic governing the interwoven flow of carries, tosses, and catches.

Lucky reader! **You** won't have to search for the pattern. I've laid out all the moves (six of them; three and their reverse) for you. If (ideally) you've already learned Burke's Barrage, you're ready for this one. It's not an easy trick to learn, but it's worth the effort because, whereas some juggling tricks are notable for their difficulty and others for their beauty, this trick has both!

Start with two balls in the right hand, one in the left.

1. RH tosses ① up at the right middle of the juggle space. (This is a starting move only. The ongoing juggle is comprised of Steps 2-7.)

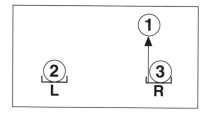

2. LH tosses ② (which will "tennis" back and forth throughout) to the right, claws ① down, crossing **over** the right arm, and starts a counter-clockwise "wheel" carry (so far, just like Burke's Barrage).

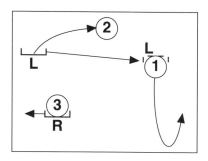

---

†Rick Rubenstein invented this trick. "Revenge" I took from Rubik's second, equally perplexing, cube of the same name.

3. RH tosses ③ straight up on the **left** side of the juggle space, then goes rightward to catch ②. Then RH immediately begins a quick counter-clockwise carry that will travel in a full circle over, under, and around the next ball to be tossed. (This "circle" carry occurs in the Two-Hand Weave (p. 60) also.) Meanwhile, LH is "wheeling."

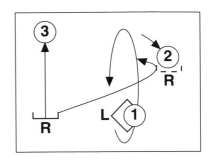

4. LH, completing its "wheel" carry, arcs ① up toward the centre (this is the ball RH "circles"); then catches ③ at the left.

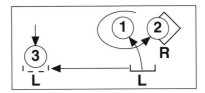

5. RH completes the full circle carry of ② around the ascending ①, tennises ② to the left and claws ① down and across the juggle space, over the left arm, to begin a leftside, clockwise "wheel" carry (as in Burke's Barrage).

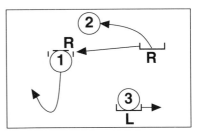

6. LH tosses ③ straight up on the **right** side of the juggle space, then goes leftward to catch ②. Then it immediately begins a quick clockwise carry that will travel in a full circle over, under, and around the next ball to be tossed. (Meanwhile, RH is "wheeling.")

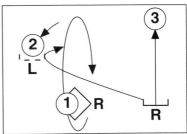

7. RH, completing its "wheel" carry, arcs ① up toward the centre (this is the ball LH "circles"); then catches ③ at the right.

Now continue by repeating Steps 2-7.

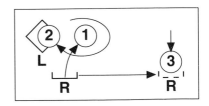

Note: In the Revenge, as in the Barrage, ② is always the "tennis" ball, but ① and ③ continually change hands. More specifically, ① is always the "wheel" ball, and ③ is always the ball that gets thrown straight up on either side. And one more difference – neither hand makes two consecutive throws – i.e., the throws alternate R-L-R-L-R-L and so on.

* *

Then there's the juggler who died and went to
Hell – but he made a deal with the Devil to come
back for one last fling!

* *

Chapter 6

Flashy Stuff

How many different ways can you throw 3 balls up in the air and catch them? A fascinating question. This chapter presents a wide variety of ingenious 3-ball juggling inventions – each one a tribute to the imagination of a fellow juggler – and yet it's probably just the start of a beginning of a partial listing. I've heard of someone with a file-card collection of 500 3-ball tricks!

In the following chapter, the balls fly in all directions – behind your back, over your shoulder, under your leg, behind your neck, leisurely, speedily, and sometimes in ways that seem impossible. You'll learn the **throws** in no time; the catch, of course, is learning to make the **catches**!

Tough challenges lie beyond, but also some satisfying moments of triumph. So, pick a trick – something really flashy – and juggle on!

* *

Like worlds in an orbital
   system,
As you cross 'em and
   weave 'em and twist 'em,
Juggling balls whirl in time
To a rhythm sublime
Then it all turns to mud
   'cuz you missed 'em.

* *

Back Cross

In this trick, the only variation from the Cascade pattern is the flight path of a single ball. When cascading, the usual right hand throw leads to the usual left hand catch, but now, instead of cascading the ball **across the front** of your body, you reach your right hand **behind your back** and throw the ball over your left shoulder to that same left hand catch. Though I'm sure the foregoing is, theoretically, crystal clear, it may take a bit of practice before your body catches up with your mind! So here's the best way to learn:

First, practice with just one ball, the right hand throwing "a back cross" for a left-hand catch.

Afterward, when you've got some control of the throw, hold two balls in the right hand, one in the left. Then, begin a Cascade with a "back cross" throw.

1. RH ① back crosses, and, as it crosses over the left shoulder...

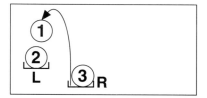

2. LH cascades ②, then catches ① and a Cascade is underway.

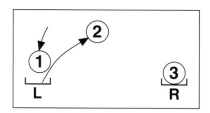

Eventually, try getting a Cascade started first. Then, when it's time for a LH throw...

1. LH cascades ① extra high (to give the RH time to catch it after the back cross throw) and catches ③.

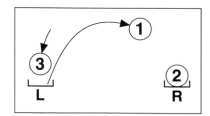

2. RH back crosses ②, then scoots around quickly to the front to catch ①.

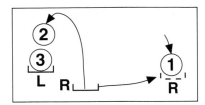

3. LH cascades ③ and catches ②... Cascade continues.

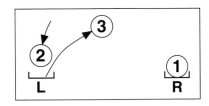

Now you've got all the info you need. Remember, it's not a complicated trick; it's just not like anything you've ever asked your body to do before. Of course, you'll also want to learn to make back crosses with your left hand, so just reverse the instructions above.

The Flip

A "flip" is a toss, back to front, over the shoulder of the hand that does the throwing. As you cascade, your **right hand** reaches behind you, fingers pointing back, and flips the ball up and over your **right** shoulder for a catch in the front. As for the catch, you have a choice—you can flip the ball **straight** over for a right-hand catch, or direct the ball **leftward** for a left-hand catch. In the latter case, your Cascade would be uninterrupted; the ball has simply followed a fancier flight path from the right hand to the left. If you flip **straight** over, just cascade the ball you are holding in your right hand over to the left, then catch the ball you flipped.

* *

Which juggling trick is like a brassiere?
The one with the catch behind the back.

* *

INTRODUCING "FLIP" AND "ZIP"

Some names are inevitable. For instance, we use a **flip** of the wrist when we make a "flip" – a **back-to-front** throw with the **right** hand over the **right** shoulder, or with the **left** hand over the **left** shoulder. That makes "flip" the natural name for this kind of throw. It also helps us distinguish it from that other throw called the "back cross" in which the **right-hand** throw comes over the **left** shoulder (or, conversely, a **left-hand** throw comes over the **right** shoulder). Having two different names for these moves can avoid confusion when talking or writing about them.

Similarly, "zip" seems to describe perfectly the short, speedy **horizontal throw** used in such patterns as the Shower, the See Saw, the Double Box, and others. Consulting the dictionary, I found "zippy" defined as "brisk" or "snappy" – and since that's just what a fast horizontal throw is, I say let's call it a "zip"!

Flipping Two

While cascading, don't throw the ball in your right hand when a throw is due; instead, hold on to it and claw-catch the ball incoming from the left. Now you've got two balls in your right hand. Continue the downward motion of the claw-catch and carry both balls behind your back for a "flip" (over the same shoulder). **But, first** (and here's the thrill move), throw the ball that's in your left hand up the centre; **then** flip the pair that's in your right hand, aiming for the midpoint of the juggle space. (Keep your middle finger in between the two balls when you throw and they should separate as they fly.) While they're coming over, catch the single ball and send it back up again. Then catch the pair, one in each hand, and toss one across to resume your Cascade.

You can also use this move as a start: Hold two balls in your right hand, one in your left, and begin where I say "**But, first**" in the paragraph above. Additionally, a **behind-the-back** throw can substitute for the **flip**. Either way, it's a winner!

Behind-the-back Catch

There is a touch of magic in a Behind-the-Back Catch. You recklessly throw a ball back over your shoulder— out of sight! – then coolly, blindly, and amazingly you casually reach back and snag the ball! Magic, what else?

Actually, by eyeing the flight of the ball as it crosses over your shoulder, it's fairly easy (with practice) to gauge where it's heading and catch it. (And if you know some magic words, it won't hurt to say them.)

In the middle of a Cascade...

1. LH throws ① over your **right** shoulder, aiming it to fall straight down behind the right arm, then catches ③.

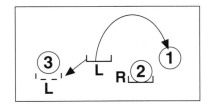

2. RH cascades ②, then quickly reaches behind to catch ① at about hip height, and brings it around to the front to continue the Cascade.

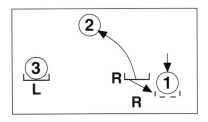

If you like this kind of behind-the-back hocus pocus, there's more to come, particularly the Toss Over the Same Shoulder (p. 76).

CATCH BEHIND THE BACK – WAYS TO RETURN

After you catch a ball behind your back, you can return it to the Cascade in a variety of ways other than a simple carry to the front. Here are four:

1. **Flip** it back over the same shoulder.

2. Do a **behind-the-back throw** over the other shoulder.

3. A behind-the-back catch with the right hand will lead smoothly to a return throw from under the right leg.

4. Similarly, a ball caught in back with the left hand can reappear from under the right armpit!

Toss Over The Same Shoulder

You're doing a Cascade; then, when it's time for a right-hand throw, instead of the usual toss **across** to the left hand, you toss the ball straight back over your **right** shoulder for a **right**-hand, behind-the-back catch – "right to right" in juggler's jargon. Since the Cascade pattern has been radically altered, what happens now to the other balls? Follow the action step by step and find out.

Cascade, then…

1. RH tosses ① directly over the **right** shoulder and catches incoming ②.

2. RH immediately throws ② back to the LH and is thus free to reach behind the back and catch ①. Notice that you've made **two consecutive RH throws**.

3. LH cascades ③ and catches ②.

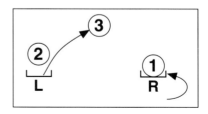

The right hand then comes back around to the front and the Cascade can be resumed.

You can also expand this manoeuvre to alternate right- and left-side tosses over the same shoulder by using the following cadence – "TOSS-2-3-4, TOSS-2-3- 4" – wherein "TOSS" means a Toss Over the Same Shoulder and "2-3-4" are regular Cascade throws. Keep in mind that "TOSS" and "2" will be throws with the same hand.

A third variation is also possible, but a lot tougher. **Every other** throw is a toss over the same shoulder. The cadence is: right hand "TOSS-2," (two RH throws) then left hand "TOSS-2" (two LH throws). One ball tennises back and forth. The TOSS-ed balls each remain in their respective hands throughout. Mighty impressive, when it's working.

One Ball Handed Behind The Back

This trick is similar to the 3-Ball Flash (p. 8), but only two balls get tossed high and in quick succession. The third ball is handed or zipped (short-tossed) behind the back. There are two patterns for this trick.

STRAIGHT-UP VARIATION

Start a Cascade, then…

1. RH tosses ① straight up about 4-5 feet, then catches the incoming ball, ③.

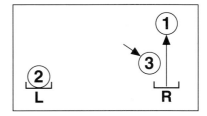

2. LH, just a split second later, tosses ② straight up about 4-5 feet (no ball to catch).

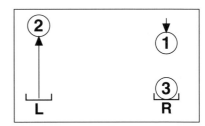

3. RH, reaching behind the back, hands ③ to LH, then catches ①.

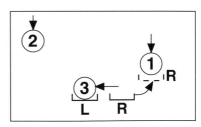

4. LH cascades ③ and catches ②.

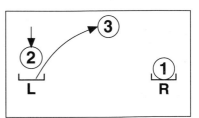

CASCADE VARIATION

Start a Cascade, then...

1. RH cascades ① about 5-6 feet high, then catches the incoming ball.

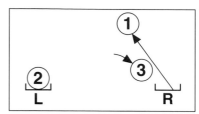

2. LH, a split second later, cascades ② up about 5-6 feet.

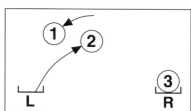

3. RH speedily hands ③ behind the back into the LH (no ball to catch).

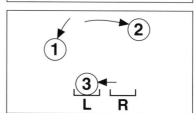

4. LH brings ③ to the front, quickly makes a normal cascade throw to the right and catches ①.

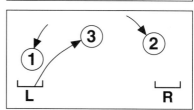

5. RH catches ②, immediately cascades it leftward and catches ③.

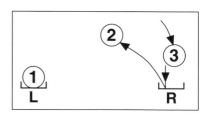

Cascade resumes.

Exchange Behind The Back

Let's say that, with just one ball, you have been practicing a right-hand throw over the left shoulder for a right-hand, behind-the-back catch. When you've got this catch fairly under control, you can try an Exchange Behind the Back, an "exchange" being a one-hand, **simultaneous** catch and throw. Here's what you do:

Cascade, then...

1. RH throws ① over the left shoulder and catches ② incoming from the right.

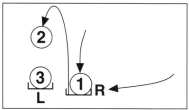

2. While ① is crossing over your left shoulder, RH brings ② around behind your back and throws it over your left shoulder (for a LH catch) and, **at the very same instant**, catches ① descending behind your back.

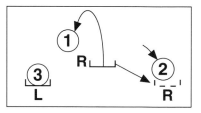

Note that you do not first throw ② and then catch ①. With the same upward movement of the right hand, you **simultaneously** throw ② off your fingertips and catch ① in your palm.

It's not as difficult as it sounds, and neither is the armpit variation, in which the right hand aims ① so that it will drop to a point just in front of the left shoulder. The right hand then catches ②, and, as you lean back slightly, carries ② around your back to make an exchange of ① and ② with ② emerging, in front, from just under the left armpit. This variation is also preparation for the Under-the-Arm Cascade, in which the right hand remains in the around-the-back position and you cascade in the space under the left armpit(!).

Fake Slam

Raise your right hand as if to slam (see The Slam, p. 36) a ball across. Instead of slamming it and catching the rising ball, use the ball you're holding, the heel of your palm, your wrist, or your forearm to slam (it's more like a slap, actually) the rising ball back toward the hand it just left. Reverse cascade with that hand, catch the slammed ball, and resume a regular Cascade.

This variation works well with the Slam Exchange (p. 58), too.

Drop Behind The Back

In this manoeuvre you vary just one Cascade throw – but what a bold variation!

Cascade, then...

1. In place of a normal Cascade throw, LH quickly reaches back, holds ① in back of the neck, and drops it straight down behind the back, then goes back to the front to catch the ball incoming from the right.

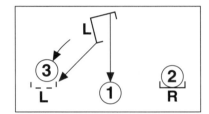

2. RH cascades ②, quickly reaches around behind the back for a blind catch of ① (practice required, obviously), and returns to the front.

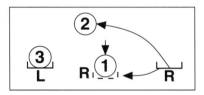

Resume a normal Cascade.

Back To Front Crossover (One Side Only)

This is a very flashy manoeuvre – at one point the balls seem to be totally out of control and flying in all directions. But, miraculously, the chaos resolves itself as you casually make all the required catches and resume the original pattern.

To warm up, start with a "columns" juggle. Then, when when the centre ball is in the air and it's time to throw the two "outside" balls, do a Crossover – that is, throw the two outside balls so that they cross over the top of the juggle space and land in the opposite column. Then do another Crossover, but with this difference – flip one of the balls from behind your back. Specifically, after you've thrown up the centre ball...

1a. RH flips ①, back to front, over the **right** shoulder aiming for a **left**-side LH catch, even as...

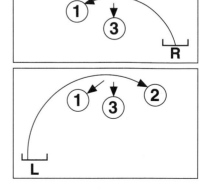

1b. LH, simultaneously, in front, reverse cascades ② high over the descending ③, aiming for a right-side, right-hand catch. (① and ② cross over.)

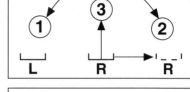

2. RH (or LH – both hands are free at this point), catches ③ and sends it back up the middle column.

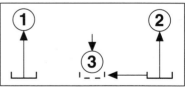

3. LH catches ①, and RH catches ②, then both throw balls straight up and the columns juggle resumes.

You can also do this trick in the middle of a Cascade. Just throw one ball up the middle; then toss the other two in a Back to Front Crossover, as above.

Or, as you cascade, try throwing one ball over your shoulder for a behind-the-back catch; throw the second ball up the middle and you're in position for a Back to Front Crossover of the next two balls.

Two Consecutive Balls Over The Same Shoulder

If you have developed some proficiency with both "behind-the-back" and "flip" throws, you might want to put them both to work in the same trick. In the middle of a Cascade, two balls can be made to pop up, one after another, from behind your back **over the same shoulder**! That second ball seems to come out of nowhere. Here's how you do it. While cascading...

1. RH "flips" ① (back to front over the **right** shoulder) aiming for a **left**-handed catch, then, in front, catches the ball incoming from the left.

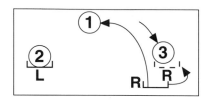

2. LH throws ② behind the back to follow ① over the right shoulder, but aiming for a **right**-handed catch, then, in front, catches ①.

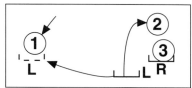

3. RH cascades ③, catches ② and a normal juggle is resumed.

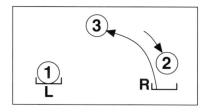

You might want to practice at first with just two balls. Hold one in each hand, then…

1. RH flips ① over the right shoulder aiming for a left-handed catch.

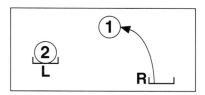

2. LH throws ② behind the back, over the right shoulder, aiming for a right-handed catch. LH catches ①, RH catches ②.

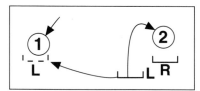

Now reverse the pattern and flip ① over the left shoulder with the left hand aiming for a **right**-handed catch, and follow with a right hand behind-the-back throw of ②, aiming for a **left**-handed catch. The right hand catches ① and the left hand catches ②.

Keep it going. It's a great way to practice these two kinds of back-to-front throws.

Behind The Neck

As you cascade, you can send one of the balls along a daring detour by lowering your head slightly and skimming a ball just over the back of your neck for a catch in front with the other hand. If you turn your body a bit to the right as you make a **right-hand** throw, and then rotate to the left as the ball crosses over behind your neck, you'll create the illusion that the ball was headed **behind your back** but mysteriously **curved around to the front** for the left-hand catch.

More than in other juggles, the trick here is to "groove the throw." This is a "blind" throw: there's no time to watch the throw or make adjustments for the catch, so the ball must simply drop unerringly into your hand at the same point in space every time. (This may sound difficult, but, in fact, after the 2,000th practice throw, it'll seem much easier; then you can start practicing left-hand throws.)

The trick can be performed using either a Cascade **or** a Half Shower pattern. In a Cascade, you simply replace a normal Cascade throw with a Behind-the-Neck throw. With the Half Shower, you can make one or **every** throw go behind the neck. The Long Throw variation (described next) is based on the Half Shower pattern.

The Long Throw

Here's how my friend Gary does the Behind-the-Neck juggle. You've got to see it to believe it, and even then you might not! Get this: He stretches both hands wide, fastens his gaze (throughout!) on his **right hand**, and commences a Half Shower with his left hand making a long throw of each ball, one after the other, **behind his neck** to a right-hand catch. That hand then returns each ball in another long throw across his chest to a **blind catch** with the left hand! The staggering combination of difficulties – the **long throw** that goes **behind the neck**, the **split second** to spot the ball just before the right-hand catch, and the **blind left-hand catch** – makes you think you're witnessing some sort of miracle!

Again, the secret is a throw that is very "grooved." Other than that, I'd suggest clean living, plenty of rest, endless practice, a balanced diet, and if you're still in trouble, call Gary at 1-800-JUG-HELP!

The Take Out

No reference to food here – this is a move, not a meal. But it may well increase your appetite – for juggling!

Hold two balls in the left hand and one in the right with right palm facing down.

1. LH throws ① and ② straight up in a "stack" (one ball directly above the other), and, simultaneously, RH places ③ in the now-empty LH.

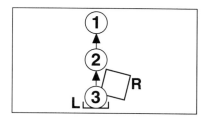

2. RH, in a shoulder-high, horizontal sweep outward from the body, "takes out" (claw-catches and carries) ②, the lower ball in the stack.

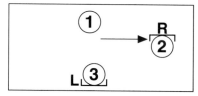

3. Finally, LH catches ①. It is now holding two balls, ready for another "stack" throw.

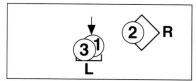

Repeat the sequence continuously for an ongoing juggle.

Stack and Carry Start

Here's a slow, mysterious start with a distinct sleight-of-hand effect just to let your audience know right from the start that they're in the hands of a master 3-ball magician.

Start with one ball in the right hand, two in the left.

1. RH cascades ① over to the midpoint.

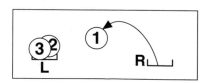

2. LH tosses ② and ③ about a foot straight up in a vertical "stack" at the left middle of the juggle space and immediately catches ①.

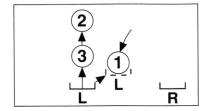

3. RH (empty) swoops across to catch ③, the lower ball in the stack, and carry it over the left arm to the far left side of the juggle space.

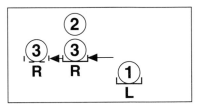

4. LH tosses ① under the right arm, straight up at the right middle of the juggle space, and, still under the right arm, catches descending ② (the top ball in the stack).

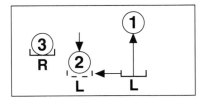

5. RH still at the far left, tosses ③ straight up and catches ① back at the right.

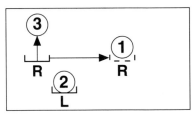

6. LH cascades ②, catches ③ and a Cascade is underway.

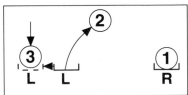

Under-the-leg Catch

As you cascade, aim a left-hand throw so that ① falls, close to your body, straight down the middle of the juggle space; then catch the incoming ball.

Next, as the right hand throws ② straight up, raise your right leg and reach under it to catch ①.

The right hand then cascades ①, catches ② and the Cascade is resumed.

Alternatively, instead of tossing ② **straight up**, you can **reverse cascade** it to the left over the raised leg and then catch ①. It's a bit more difficult, but you may prefer this variation. Or, as you cascade, the right hand can toss ① straight up, then catch the incoming ball. Then the left hand will cascade and reach under the right leg to catch ① at the far right. A normal Cascade follows.

Back-of-the-hand Catch and Toss

The catch is a "soft" catch, the back of the hand rising to meet the ball and ease it down; and it's also a "fork" catch, wherein the ball settles into the convenient groove created by curving up the forefinger and ring finger and depressing the middle finger. Before continuing, you might want to practice this "fork" catch using just one ball. Besides this unusual catch, I want to alert you to an important effect at Step 2. As the right hand lifts the ball for a back-of-the-hand throw, a ball from the left hand comes rising up beneath it, following the first ball, like two elevator cars ascending on the same vertical track. The audience's collective eye is caught, held, mesmerised, delighted. Quick! Pass the hat!

(NOTE: The diagrams for this trick, and for the "fork" juggles that follow, show the fork in profile, even though the fingers actually point to the front.)

1. While you are cascading, RH throws ① and catches the incoming ③ on the back of the hand.

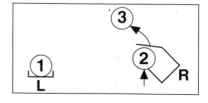

The next two throws are performed simultaneously.

2a. LH tosses ② straight up under the RH and catches ①, even as...

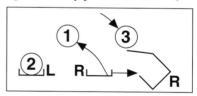

2b. RH tosses ③ to the left with a lifting movement that resembles a Reverse Cascade throw, then claw-catches ② rising up directly beneath it.

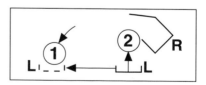

Now, either resume the Cascade, or repeat the Back-of-the-Hand Catch and Toss as many times as you wish.

BACK OF THE HAND CASCADE

More difficult than a single catch and toss is a sustained Cascade pattern with all catches being made on the backs of both hands. Using the three-finger catch described above, first practice with just one hand making back-of-the-hand catches. When you've mastered the skill with one hand, switch to the other, then try both together. It's a tough trick and as the young man who showed it to me remarked, it'll take "many hours over the bed."

Fork Catch and Resume Cascade

This is not a difficult trick, but it requires some proficiency at making a "fork" catch on the back of your fingers, a skill you'll also need for some of the tricks that follow. This charming little change-up, stop-and-start move gives you a great chance to practice the fork catch. Here the fork catch will be made on the right hand (and won't your mom be pleased that you're using the right fork).

1. Pause in your Cascade and make a "fork" catch of ① on the back of the extended first two fingers of the RH. You should now have a ball in each palm and one on the RH "fork."

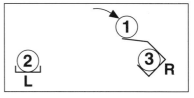

2. After about a 2-second pause, turn your RH sideways, pointing it towards the LH, and, with your LH, reverse cascade ② over to the right.

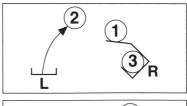

3. When ② has crossed about two-thirds over the juggle space, RH tosses up both balls at the juggle midpoint, angling ①, from atop the "fork," back toward the right, and ③, from the palm, over to the left. The RH catches ② and LH catches ③.

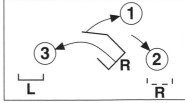

(continued on next page)

4. RH cascades ② and catches ①.

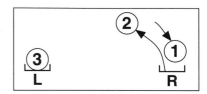

Resume the Cascade.

Fork Juggles

Here are two small-scale but fascinating juggles that feature fork catches (as in the diagrams for the last two tricks, the "forks" are shown in profile, even though the fingers actually point forward). Both start with a ball in each hand and the third ball perched on the back of the extended first and second fingers of one hand – the so-called "fork." The first juggle, The Twist, is very much like a little dance.

THE TWIST

The right hand holds two balls, one in the palm and one on the fork. The left hand holds the third in the palm, palm facing up. The hands are held fairly close together (5-6 inches apart). Now, get ready to Twist.

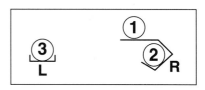

1a. RH lifts and twists palm up. The lift throws the fork- held ① straight up, about 6-7 inches. The twisting movement sends ② from the palm over to the LH, and puts the RH in position to catch ① as it falls.

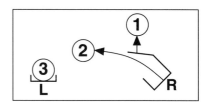

1b. As RH twists palm up, LH, simultaneously, twists palm down and catches ② on its fork. At the same moment, RH catches ①.

2a. Now reverse the throws: LH lifts and twists palm up. The lift throws fork-held ② straight up about 6-7 inches. The twist throws ③ from the palm over to the RH, and gets the LH ready to catch ② as it falls.

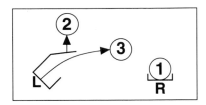

2b. RH twists palm down and catches ③ on its fork. At the same moment, LH catches ②.

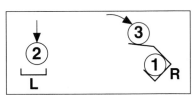

Then repeat Steps 1 and 2, and so on.

THE TOSS-UP

The right hand holds two balls, one in the palm and one on the fork. The left hand holds a ball in the palm, palm facing down. In this juggle, unlike The Twist, the palms will face downward throughout.

1a. Bring the RH in under the LH and with simultaneous throws, LH tosses ① straight up 5-6 inches (palm does **not** turn face up to throw) and RH tosses ② from the fork up towards the left palm.

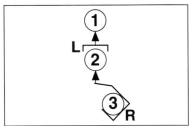

1b. LH then claws ② and catches ① on the fork.

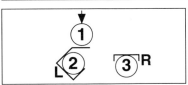

(continued on next page)

* *

The problem with juggling is that
the balls go where you throw them.

* *

NOTE: During the moves in Step 1., ③ stays in the palm of RH throughout, just as ② will stay in the palm of LH throughout Step 2.

2a. Now do the reverse: LH moves in under the RH. RH (palm down) throws ③ straight up and simultaneously, LH throws ① up towards the right palm.

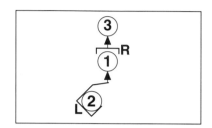

2b. RH claws ① in the palm and catches ③ on its fork.

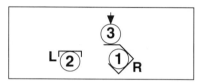

…and so on. When performed smoothly and quickly, both of these fork juggles are positively hypnotic.

Two-ball Fork Exchange

You'll need to know the Two-Ball Fork Exchange before you can learn the flashier Three-Ball variation. The Two-Ball Fork Exchange is done with one hand. Note that, although we show a side-view of the hands in the diagrams for the Two- and Three-Ball Fork Exchanges (as we've done in the preceding "fork" tricks), the fingers actually point straight forward, away from your body.

1. Hold ① in the palm with your ring, little finger, and thumb, palm facing down, and place ② on the "fork" formed by extending your forefinger and middle finger, fingers pointing forward.

2. Now flip your hand back toward your body and toss both balls in the air simultaneously – ① straight up and ② on an angle slightly back towards yourself.

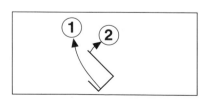

3. Reach up and quickly claw ② down and, in one continuous motion, swoop under and "soft"-catch descending ① on the fork.

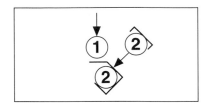

You're now in the same position as when you started, but the balls have switched places. Practice this manoeuvre until you can exchange the balls smoothly and repeatedly. When you're proficient at the Two-Ball Fork Exchange, you'll be ready to expand it into the following Three-Ball variation.

Three-ball Fork Exchange

Although I learned this trick in New York City, I have refrained from calling it the "New York Fork Exchange."

1. Hold ① and ② in the RH as above. LH holds ③ in position about 4-5 inches directly above ②.

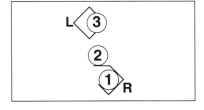

2. Now throw all three balls at once in the following directions: arc ① to the left for a claw-catch by the LH; send ② slightly up and back (as in the Two-Ball Exchange) to be quickly clawed down by the RH; toss ③ straight up about a foot for a "soft"-catch on the RH fork.

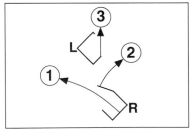

3. If you caught the balls as described in Step 2, ① is now in the LH, ② is in the palm of the RH, and ③ is on the RH fork.

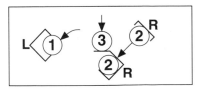

Repeat 3-4 times.

This observation will clarify the Three-Ball Fork Exchange pattern: Look at the diagram for Step 1. The balls follow each other in rotation. ③—the high ball—moves **down** to replace ② on the right hand fork; ② moves **down** to replace ① in the right hand palm; and ① moves **"up"** to replace ③ in the left hand.

Triple Claw

This trick has that mysterious look of levitation that is one of the basic delights in juggling. One hand does a quick back-and-forth series of "claw" catches, creating the illusion of a ball suspended in the air. This is bound to quicken some pulses. You might even hear a gasp or two, even some aaahhhs! (And when you hear aaahhhs, you know you're a wizard.)

Start with a Cascade, then...

1. LH throws ① over, and about 6 inches beyond the RH, then catches the ball incoming from the right.

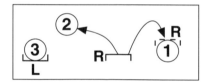

2. RH, in a palm-downward position, throws ② straight up about 4-5 inches, reaches quickly to the right and "claws" ①.

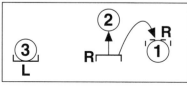

3. RH, still in action, throws ① straight up about 4-5 inches and "claws" ②.

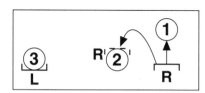

4. RH, still in a blur of activity, throws ② toward the LH and "claws" ① again. Now turn the RH palm up as LH resumes a Cascade.

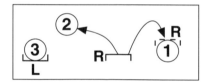

Since these are fairly rapid moves, you might want to practice "clawing," using a 2-in-1-Hand pattern and making all "claw" catches and "claw" throws. This will give you the skill needed for the three speedy "claws" in Steps 2, 3, and 4. Also, at first, it might be well to toss the "clawed" balls higher than 4-5 inches, until you have more control. Eventually, you'll be able to lower these throws to heighten the "hanging-in-the-air" effect.

Crossunder

Here's a sizzling little move, two or three repetitions of which should add considerable spice to your 3-ball routine. While doing a side-by-side columns juggle, cross your hands under the juggle and throw the balls straight up in columns on either side of the middle ball. You can then either immediately repeat this Crossunder or resume your columns juggle.

The Crossunder move is best learned as presented here – while juggling in side-by-side columns – but once you've got it you can also throw it into the middle of a Cascade as a surprise switch-up.

The Slice

When executed with precise timing, this trick produces a unique audio-visual effect. You carry a ball with a swift horizontal slicing movement under another ball that is dropping straight down through the centre of the juggle space. Suddenly, an abrupt **stop** at the end of this slicing movement is timed to coincide with the **"snap"** sound that occurs as the ball falling in the centre is caught; and, **simultaneously**, a third ball, exchanged for the ball caught, **pops** into the air. Thus, the trick creates a "stop! snap! pop!" that makes a crisp auditory as well as visual effect.

Start with a Cascade, then...

1. LH throws ① straight up about 2-3 feet at the centre of the juggle space, then catches the ball incoming from the right.

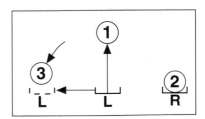

2a. RH, holding ②, swoops horizontally, from far right to far left, under the falling ① and over the left arm. Time the swoop to stop abruptly at the exact moment a "snap" is heard as LH makes its catch (described next). Note: RH makes no throw, just performs the carry.

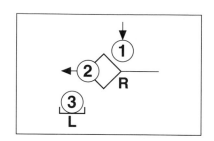

2b. LH, at the low centre of the juggle, catches ① and at the same time pops ③ into the air, up and slightly toward the right. The stop, the snap, and the pop occur simultaneously!

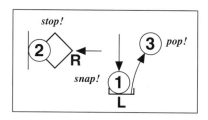

3. RH, still at the left side, tosses ② straight up, then catches ③ over on the right.

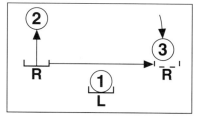

4. LH cascades ① to the right and catches ②.

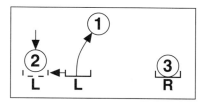

Resume the Cascade.

* *

Be careful – juggling is catching!

* *

CONTINUOUS SLICING

A pattern with Continuous Slicing can be created by changing Step 3 as follows:

3a. RH, at the left side and **palm facing down**, in one movement to the right, drops ② towards the LH at the centre of the juggle, and reaches to claw-catch ③ over on the right. And, simultaneously...

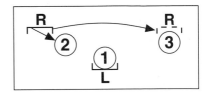

3b. LH tosses ① straight up the centre of the juggle space just after RH crosses over, and catches ② at the same moment that RH claws ③ (above).

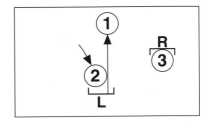

4. RH swoops across for the "stop! snap! pop!" effect (a repeat of Steps 2a and 2b).

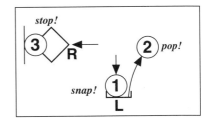

And so on.

When you've got the trick working, you'll notice that the vertical left-hand tosses and the horizontal right-hand carries combine to produce a unique cross- shaped pattern.

Reachover, Claw, and Whiparound

I acknowledge that the name is unwieldy, but it describes exactly what you must do—reach high over the juggle space, claw a ball at its peak, and whip it back around. Learn the trick and then, if you wish, rename it; no hard feelings.

Cascade, and when it's time for the left hand to throw...

1. LH throws ① straight up about 8 inches and catches the ball incoming from the right.

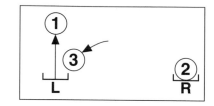

2. RH arcs high over the juggle space, carrying ② and releasing it about a third of the way across in a **sort of** reverse cascade throw, and, continuing the arc, claws ① at its peak.

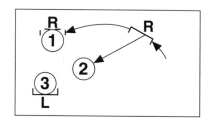

3. LH launches ③ in a short straight throw up the middle, then catches ② at left.

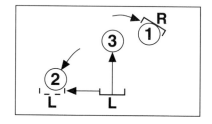

4. RH, after claw-catching ①, immediately retraces the arc at high speed, whipping the ball over and down and moving smoothly into a cascade toss under ③ (a nice effect!) to resume the pattern, then catches ③.

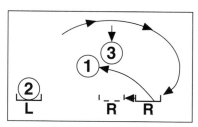

The Disappearing Ball

This is a true magician's stunt, but the magician must also be a juggler. While doing a counterclockwise 2-in-1-Hand pattern with your left hand, you pass a right-hand-held ball in a circle 2 or 3 times over and under **every other ball** that's thrown. But, after one of these passes, your right hand is suddenly empty – the ball has disappeared! Another circle or two through the juggle with the empty hand and the ball reappears. Here's how it's done:

Start a counterclockwise 2-in-1-Hand juggle in the left hand with ① and ②. Hold ③ in the right hand, visible to the audience.

1. As LH tosses ① up counter-clockwise, RH carries ③ in a circle, also counterclockwise, over and under ①. LH catches ②.

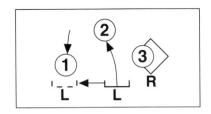

2. LH tosses ② up counterclockwise and catches ①.

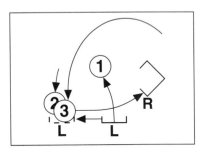

Repeat Steps 1 and 2 several times, but then...

3. As you carry ③ over ① and down, place ③ in the back part of your left hand, leaving your fingers free to catch ② and continue the 2-in-1-Hand juggle. Keep making circular RH carries, but now the audience will see that your hand is empty; ③ will be riding along in the LH virtually invisible because the hand is in constant motion.

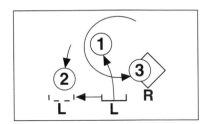

4. After two or three "empty" carries over ①, LH releases both ② and ③ and RH claw-catches ③ as it swings through its arc. The effect created is that the missing ball has mysteriously reappeared!

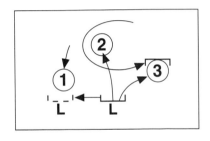

Hand Rolling

"Hand Rolling" means making three balls go around and around in the palm of your hand. No throwing, no catching; the skill here is finger manipulation.

The balls can be rolled either clockwise or counterclockwise. For a **right-hand counterclockwise** rotation place ① at position P (for palm); ② at position L (for little finger); and ③ at position F (for forefinger). Position T (for thumb) remains empty.

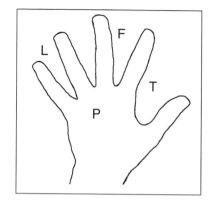

IMPORTANT

1. Always move all three balls **simultaneously**.

2. Move the balls in a **large** circle so that they **do not touch**.

Start by tilting your hand slightly to the right to roll ① from P to T. Simultaneously, with the fingers, coax ② from L to P, and ③ from F to L. Finally, with the thumb, give ① an extra little push to roll it **through** position T to F. That completes one "shift".

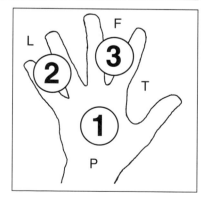

At first, practice the shifts one at a time, striving for simultaneous movement and no touching. The goal will be to eventually merge consecutive shifts into a continuous seamless flow, the balls moving smoothly around and around like bottles on a factory conveyor.

Right-hand **clockwise** rotation will require a different initial positioning of the balls. (You might find that some other initial positioning works better for you. By all means, use it.)

Place ① at T; ② at F; and ③ at L. Then, **simultaneously**, shift ① to P, coax ② to T, and ③ over to F. Finally, keep ① rolling through position P to L. That completes the shift.

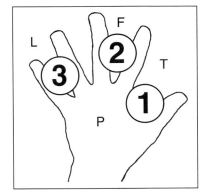

To "hand roll" with the left hand, reverse the above directions for the right hand. Also, an excellent preparation for 3-ball hand rolling is 2-ball hand rolling. In this simpler version, specific positions are not crucial, but it is still important to make a **large** circle so that the balls **do not touch**. That's the **roll'em desideratum!**

Chapter 7

Beyond Three Balls

Someday, if you haven't already started, you will probably take up the challenge of four- and five-ball juggling. Not only will this be a new level for you in terms of the number of balls you'll be throwing, but the actual **height of each toss** will also be on a new level, at least twice as high as the usual chest-high three-ball patterns.

Your main task then, as you move "up" in juggling, will be to develop the control needed to keep your throws consistently even at this new four- and five- ball height. To help gain this control, the following three-ball tricks, which I call "transition tricks," will be of great value, because, though only three balls are used, they must be thrown at four- and five-ball heights. Perfecting **these** tricks should smooth your transition into performing four- and five-ball patterns.

High Shower

In a regular Shower pattern (see p. 4), throw the balls higher than normal, to a point at least a foot over your head. Throw both clockwise and counter-clockwise to give practice to both hands.

High Cascade

Do the regular ol' Cascade, but this time throw the balls a foot or more over your head. Select a specific height and try to hit that level with every throw. Also try a low Cascade that gradually builds in height and then diminishes, up and down, over and over, as a fountain might.

Three-ball Flash

Review this move (p. 8) and practice starting with each hand.

The Snake

This trick is excellent preparation for learning to do the the Five-Ball Cascade. The Snake uses only three balls but tosses them in the five-ball pattern.

When starting the Five-Ball Cascade, the right hand holds three balls, the left hand two, and the first five tosses are R, L, R, L, R. By eliminating the two left hand balls, we derive the Snake pattern; that is, using the same timing, the right hand tosses the three balls consecutively in a high arc over to the left. Then the left hand consecutively catches and returns the balls, in a similar high arc, back to the right.

Since there are two balls missing from this essentially five-ball pattern, you must pause in your timing where these throws would normally occur. Therefore, you might want to use the following cadence as you throw, with "and" indicating a pause for a throw of one of the "missing" balls, and no pause between ③ and ①, which is a normal Five-Ball right-left or left-right. Here's the cadence:

① and ② and ③ ① and ② and ③ ① and ② and ③

Note: You catch ① a split second before you throw ③.

* *

Juggler: My next trick is so unbelievably difficult,
I'm not even gonna try it!

* *

About the Author

George Gillson, artist and writer, now proudly adds "amateur juggler" to his list of accomplishments. He lives and works in New York City and is a regular at the now-famous Carmine Street Gym Thursday night juggling session (don't miss it if you're in New York). He has spent the last four years learning about juggling and collecting the best 3-ball tricks he could find, and, when juggler-writer met juggler-editor Larry Swanson, this book became the happy inevitability.

Index

Resources

For further information about Juggling and New Circus Events, Workshops, Conventions and suppliers of equipment:

International Jugglers Association (IJA)

Membership of the IJA gives an international perspective through it's quarterly magazine *Jugglers World*.
For details contact: International Jugglers Association, P.O. Box 3707 JB, Akron, OH 44314-3704, U.S.A.

Kaskade

European Juggling magazine published quarterly in English and German.
For subscriptions contact: Gabi & Paul Keast, Annastr. 7, W-6200 Wiesbaden, Germany.

The Catch

Quarterly British Magazine of Juggling, New Circus and Street Theatre.
For subscriptions contact: The Catch, Moorledge Farm Cottage, Knowle Hill, Chew Magna, Bristol BS18 8TL, England.